CL

DICK!

1001 WAYS TO BE A CHEEKY DEVIL

Also available in Beaver by John Hegarty

A VERY MICE JOKE BOOK
NOT THE ELEPHANT JOKE BOOK
A JUMBLE OF JUNGLY JOKES

CLEVER DICK!

1001 WAYS TO BE A CHEEKY DEVIL

John Hegarty

Illustrated by David Mostyn

BEAVER BOOKS

A Beaver Book
Published by Arrow Books Limited
62–5 Chandos Place, London WC2N 4NW

An imprint of Century Hutchinson Ltd

London Melbourne Sydney Auckland
Johannesburg and agencies throughout the world

First published 1988

Text © Martyn Forrester 1988
Illustrations © David Mostyn 1988

Set in Century Schoolbook
by JH Graphics Ltd, Reading

Made and printed in Great Britain
by Anchor Brendon Ltd
Tiptree, Essex

ISBN 0 09 956280 4

Contents

Introduction   7

Rules   8

1 Clever Dick at Home   11

2 Clever Dick at School   78

3 Clever Dick at Large   119

For Richard

Introduction

The trouble with the world today is that people aren't cheeky enough to each other.

When Mikhail Gorbachev meets the President of the United States, he should say: 'I'm sure we've met before. I don't remember your name, but I never forget a big nose.'

And when the Russian leader asks: 'What do you think of the space programme?', Ronald Reagan ought to be a Clever Dick and say: 'I don't know, I never watch it.'

Likewise when Neil Kinnock meets the Prime Minister, he should say: 'Margaret, your face looks like a million dollars . . . all green and wrinkled.'

And when he asks her what she thinks of private enterprise, Margaret Thatcher ought to say, quick as a flash: 'He's OK, but I prefer Captain Kirk.'

Then they could all have a good laugh, forget all about nuclear weapons, and the world would be a better place for the rest of us Clever Dicks to live in . . .

Rules

Being a Clever Dick is great fun, but like everything else worthwhile in life, there are certain rules:

1. *DON'T* BE A CLEVER DICK unless it's fun for everyone involved: always pick on someone your own size — or preferably bigger.
2. *DON'T* BE A CLEVER DICK in front of the Queen: always let her go first.
3. *DON'T* BE A CLEVER DICK with any other member of the Royal Family (except a young one like Prince William).
4. *NEVER* BE A CLEVER DICK if it's going to hurt someone's feelings.
5. *NEVER* BE A CLEVER DICK if it's going to make someone cry.
6. *NEVER* BE A CLEVER DICK if it's going to make someone cross.
7. *NEVER* BE A CLEVER DICK with someone who is old, disabled, nervous or shy.
8. In short, *NEVER* be a Clever Dick if it's going to spoil someone's day, cause loss of life or limb, or trigger off a total global thermonuclear war.

BITS OF THE WORLD!

HOWEVER:

1. *DO* BE A CLEVER DICK with your best friends at school.
2. *DO* BE A CLEVER DICK with your brothers, sisters and parents (as long as you're wearing full protective body armour).
3. *DO* BE A CLEVER DICK with your teacher (as long as you have no ambition to stay at school and grow up clever enough to write books as amazingly intellectual as this one).

1 Clever Dick at Home

CLEVER DICK SAYS: Home is where you can say anything you like, because nobody pays any attention to you anyway.

CLEVER DICK: If I come home from school and smell a delicious meal cooking, I know one thing immediately.
FRIEND: What's that?
CLEVER DICK: I'm in the wrong house.

CLEVER DICK: I'm homesick.
MOTHER: But this is your home!
CLEVER DICK: I know, and I'm sick of it!

CLEVER DICK SAYS: Our house is so small, even the mice are round-shouldered.

CLEVER DICK SAYS: My mother changes the sheets twice a week — from one bed to the next.

FRIEND: Are the rooms quiet in your house?
CLEVER DICK: Of course. It's the people in them that are noisy.

FRIEND: Is there any water in your room?
CLEVER DICK: There was, but we had the roof fixed.

FRIEND: Do you have hot and cold water in your house?

CLEVER DICK: Yes, hot in summer and cold in winter.

CLEVER DICK SAYS: Our house is so damp that when we laid a mousetrap we caught a herring.

FRIEND: Do you have running water in your house?

CLEVER DICK: Only when it rains.

WIFE: When will you straighten out the house, dear?

CLEVER DICK HUSBAND: Why? Is it tilted?

Clever Dick when there's a Man at the Door

SISTER: There's a man outside with a nasty look on his face.

CLEVER DICK: Tell him you've already got one.

CLEVER DICK: Who is that at the door?

BROTHER: A man with a wooden leg.

CLEVER DICK: Tell him to hop it.

SISTER: There's a man at the door collecting for the Old Folks' Home.

CLEVER DICK: Tell him he can have grandma.

SISTER: There's a woman at the door with a pram.

CLEVER DICK: Tell her to push off.

12

MOTHER: There's a man at the door collecting for the children's home's swimming pool.
CLEVER DICK: Give him a glass of water.

SALESMAN ON DOORSTEP: Madam, this book will cut your housework in half.
CLEVER DICK GIRL: Good. I'll take two of them.

MOTHER: There's a man outside with a wooden leg named Smith.
CLEVER DICK: What's the name of the other leg?

Clever Dick and Home Cooking

FRIEND: Some people can cook but don't.
CLEVER DICK: My sister can't cook but does!

CLEVER DICK: I must say, the meals at your house give food for thought.
FRIEND: Really?
CLEVER DICK: Well they're certainly not fit for eating!

FRIEND: Last year my mum served a special turkey for Christmas and everyone was absolutely tickled.
CLEVER DICK: Forgot to remove the feathers, did she?

MOTHER: How many times do I have to tell you to stay away from those cakes?
CLEVER DICK: Never again, Mum – I just finished them!

13

FRIEND: Does your family keep the kitchen clean?

CLEVER DICK: Are you joking? When the toast pops out of the toaster, it takes an hour to find it!

FATHER: Dick! You eat like a pig. Do you know what a pig is?

CLEVER DICK: Yes, Dad — a hog's son.

FIRST CANNIBAL WIFE: I don't know what to make of my husband these days.

CLEVER DICK CANNIBAL WIFE: How about a casserole?

CLEVER DICK SAYS: My sister offered to cook dinner and asked me what I'd like. I told her a life insurance policy . . .

FATHER: Before we were married your mother turned my head with her good looks.

CLEVER DICK: Now she turns your stomach with her bad cooking!

CLEVER DICK SAYS: My sister has burned so much bread our toaster has been declared a fire hazard.

CLEVER DICK SAYS: My sister's cooking is very tasty. I had some last year and I can still taste it.

CLEVER DICK: Are we eating out tonight, mum?
MOTHER: No, why?
CLEVER DICK: I don't smell anything burning.

CLEVER DICK SAYS: Every time my mother has an accident in the kitchen I have to eat it for dinner . . .

CLEVER DICK: My dad and mum have a great partnership.
FRIEND: How's that?
CLEVER DICK: He earns the bread and she burns it.

MOTHER: I've been cooking for ten years.
CLEVER DICK: You ought to be done by now, then.

MOTHER: How do you like my cakes?
CLEVER DICK: Delicious! Did you buy them yourself?

FRIEND: My mother's meals melt in your mouth.
CLEVER DICK: Too bad she doesn't defrost them first.

GIRL: May I sit on your right hand at dinner?
CLEVER DICK: I may need it to eat with, but you can hold it a while.

MOTHER: How many times have I told you not to be late for dinner?
CLEVER DICK: I don't know, I thought *you* were keeping score.

MOTHER: Why do you like gravy so much?
CLEVER DICK: Because it has no bones.

FRIEND: My sister dresses to kill.
CLEVER DICK: Too bad she cooks that way as well.

Clever Dick and Mum's Best Friend

MUM'S FRIEND: I told my husband to tell me everthing he knows.
CLEVER DICK: He must have been speechless.

MUM'S FRIEND: When I get a cold I buy a bottle of whisky and in no time it's gone.
CLEVER DICK: The cold or the whisky?

MUM'S FRIEND: I'll have you know my teeth are all my own.
CLEVER DICK: You mean you've finished paying for them at last?

MUM'S FRIEND: I haven't been myself lately.
CLEVER DICK: I noticed the improvement.

MUM'S FRIEND: What's your sister going to be when she grows up?
CLEVER DICK: An old lady.

MUM'S FRIEND: Are you a good boy?
CLEVER DICK: No, I'm the sort of kid my mother won't let me play with!

MUM'S FRIEND: I admit I won't see twenty-one again.
CLEVER DICK: You wouldn't recognize it!

MUM'S FRIEND: I think I carry my age rather well, don't you?
CLEVER DICK: You should, you've had years of experience.

CLEVER DICK SAYS: Mum's friend is so old, every time she goes into an antique shop someone tries to buy her.

MUM'S FRIEND: My new baby looks just like me.
CLEVER DICK: Never mind, as long as it's healthy.

MUM'S FRIEND: Is your new baby a boy or a girl?
CLEVER DICK: Of course, what else could it be?

MUM'S FRIEND: I've more than kept my girlish figure.
CLEVER DICK: You've doubled it!

MUM'S FRIEND: My husband bought me an electric typewriter for Christmas.
CLEVER DICK: Now all he needs to find is a chair to match . . .

MUM'S FRIEND: Every time I drink hot tea I get a sharp pain in my left eye.
CLEVER DICK: Try taking the spoon out of your cup.

CLEVER DICK: That's a lovely fur coat.
MUM'S FRIEND: Thank you.
CLEVER DICK: Did you kill it yourself?

MUM'S FRIEND: My hats will never go out of style.
CLEVER DICK: No, they'll always look silly.

MUM'S FRIEND: I passed your house yesterday.
CLEVER DICK: Thanks, I appreciate it.

MUM'S FRIEND: I've got my husband to the point where he eats out of my hand.
CLEVER DICK: Saves a lot of washing up, doesn't it?

MUM'S FRIEND: Please call me a taxi.
CLEVER DICK: Okay, you're a taxi — but you look more like the back end of a bus to me.

MUM'S FRIEND: How did you find the weather while you were away?
CLEVER DICK: I just went outside and there it was.

MUM'S FRIEND: Well, I must be going home now.
CLEVER DICK: Don't leave yet — I want to forget you exactly the way you are.

CLEVER DICK: I didn't recognize you for a minute.
MUM'S FRIEND: Didn't you?
CLEVER DICK: No. It was one of the happiest minutes I've ever spent.

MUM'ST FRIEND: Do you go to school?
CLEVER DICK: No, I'm sent.

MUM'S FRIEND: Is this one of your abstract paintings?
CLEVER DICK: No, it's a mirror.

MUM'S FRIEND: Every time I'm down in the dumps I buy a new dress.
CLEVER DICK: So that's where you get those awful things from.

MUM'S FRIEND: I didn't come here to be insulted.
CLEVER DICK: Oh, where do you usually go?

MUM'S FRIEND: Do you recognize me?
CLEVER DICK: I never forget a face, but in your case I'll make an exception.

CLEVER DICK: How old are you?
MUM'S FRIEND: Pushing thirty.
CLEVER DICK: From which direction?

CLEVER DICK: You've got a face like a million dollars.
MUM'S FRIEND: Why, thank you.
CLEVER DICK: Yes, all green and wrinkled.

MUM'S FRIEND: I'll have you know that I've got the face of an eighteen-year old.
CLEVER DICK: Well give it back, you're getting it all wrinkled.

MUM'S FRIEND: How nice to see you. You haven't changed in years.
CLEVER DICK: No, the laundry's been on strike.

MUM'S FRIEND: This hat fits really well.
CLEVER DICK: Yes, but what will you do when your ears get tired?

MUM'S FRIEND: I'm nobody's fool.
CLEVER DICK: Well, maybe you can get someone to adopt you.

MUM'S FRIEND: Matches are made in Heaven.
CLEVER DICK: Really? Then why do they cost 10p a box?

MUM'S FRIEND: I'd like to see something cheap in hats.
CLEVER DICK: Put some on and look in the mirror.

MUM'S FRIEND: I've got a bad stomach.
CLEVER DICK: Well keep your coat buttoned and maybe nobody will notice.

MUM'S FRIEND: Did you hear that Freda has had her face lifted?
CLEVER DICK: Who'd want to steal an ugly mug like that?

MUM'S FRIEND: My husband is an absolute angel.
CLEVER DICK: Yes, you can tell by the way he harps on about things.

MUM'S FRIEND: Do you do the pools?
CLEVER DICK: No, it's my dog. He's not house-trained.

MUM'S FRIEND: My husband and I were happy for twenty-five years.
CLEVER DICK: And then you met.

CLEVER DICK: I'm afraid your son's spoiled.

MUM'S FRIEND: I don't think that's true.

CLEVER DICK: It is — he's just been run over by a steamroller.

MUM'S FRIEND: My husband wears my photograph over his heart. It saved his life once when someone tried to shoot him.
CLEVER DICK: I'm not surprised. Your face would stop anything.

Clever Dick and the Neighbours

CLEVER DICK: What are you going to do with all that horse manure?
NEIGHBOUR: Put it on my rhubarb.
CLEVER DICK: Really? I always have custard on mine.

NEIGHBOUR: How dare you tell everyone I'm a stupid old fool!
CLEVER DICK: Sorry, I didn't know it was a secret.

NEIGHBOUR: How did my greenhouse get smashed?
CLEVER DICK: I was cleaning my catapult and it went off.

NEIGHBOUR: Didn't you hear me hammering on your wall during your party last night?
CLEVER DICK: That's all right — we were making quite a lot of noise ourselves.

FRIEND: I hear your neighbour is rather ugly?
CLEVER DICK: Ugly? She can make her own yoghurt by staring at a pint of milk for an hour.

NEIGHBOUR: Why have you stolen my son's trumpet? You can't play it.

CLEVER DICK: But neither can he while I have it.

ANGRY NEIGHBOUR: I'll teach you to throw stones at my greenhouse!

CLEVER DICK: I wish you would. I keep missing it!

NEIGHBOUR: My son plays the violin, he's had many requests.

CLEVER DICK: Yeah, but he insists on playing anyway.

CLEVER DICK SAYS: Anyone who thinks practice makes perfect should listen to my neighbour playing the trumpet.

CLEVER DICK SAYS: My neighbour is so big he can sit around the dinner table all by himself!

NEIGHBOUR: Did you know that your dog barked all night?

CLEVER DICK: Yes, but don't worry. He sleeps all day.

NEIGHBOUR: What are you doing in my tree, young man?

CLEVER DICK: One of your apples fell down, sir, and I'm just putting it back.

Clever Dick and Mum

MOTHER: Why have you come home early?
CLEVER DICK: Illness.
MOTHER: What's the matter?
CLEVER DICK: The teacher got sick of me.

CLEVER DICK: Mum, you know that vase you always worried I would break?
MOTHER: Yes.
CLEVER DICK: Well, your worries are over.

MOTHER: How did your cookery class go today?
CLEVER DICK DAUGHTER: Not very well. I was sent out of the classroom for burning something.
MOTHER: What did you burn?
CLEVER DICK DAUGHTER: The classroom!

MOTHER: How was your first day at school?
CLEVER DICK: All right, except for a man called Sir who kept spoiling everything.

MOTHER: How did your sister get that splinter in her finger?
CLEVER DICK: She must have scratched her head.

CLEVER DICK: Mum says she doesn't want any candles on her birthday cake.
FRIEND: Why's that?
CLEVER DICK: Because on her last birthday there were so many candles, it looked like a forest fire!

MOTHER: I just don't know what to wear to the Fancy Dress party tonight.
CLEVER DICK: With your varicose veins, why not go as a road map?

MOTHER: Why did you kick your little sister in the stomach?
CLEVER DICK: I couldn't help it. She turned around too quick.

MOTHER: Are my seams on my stockings straight?
CLEVER DICK: Your seams are okay. It's your legs that are twisted.

MOTHER: Come in and have your tea, Dick. Are your feet dirty?
CLEVER DICK: Yes, but I've got my shoes on.

FRIEND: My mother is always looking in the mirror.
CLEVER DICK: Except when she's reversing out of a parking space!

CLEVER DICK: I'm going to give you a teapot for Christmas.
MOTHER: But I've already got one.
CLEVER DICK: Not any more you don't — I just dropped it!

CLEVER DICK SAYS: My dad would like to tickle my mum under the chin, but he can't decide which one.

MOTHER: Do you think I'm putting on a little weight?

CLEVER DICK: Let's put it this way: your double chin has become a treble.

FRIEND: I've heard your mother is a very decisive person.

CLEVER DICK: That's right. When she reached forty she definitely decided what she wanted to be: twenty-five!

CLEVER DICK SAYS: My mum's hands shake so much, she can thread the needle of a sewing machine when it's running!

FRIEND: My mum has never said an unkind thing about anyone.

CLEVER DICK: That's because she only talks about herself.

MOTHER: How old do you think I am?

CLEVER DICK: You don't look it!

MOTHER: I don't look thirty-five, do I?

CLEVER DICK: No, but I bet you did when you were.

MOTHER: You mustn't pull the cat's tail.

CLEVER DICK: I'm only holding it. The cat is pulling!

MOTHER: Dick, put down that axe at once!

CLEVER DICK: But Mum, I've always wanted a half-sister!

MOTHER: Dick! Stop reaching across the table like that! Haven't you got a tongue in your head?

CLEVER DICK: Yes, Mum, but my arm is longer.

MOTHER: I made two cakes for tea today. Would you like to take your pick?

CLEVER DICK: No, I'll just use a hammer and chisel.

MOTHER: Dick, why are you making faces at that warthog?

CLEVER DICK: He started it!

MOTHER: Before you eat your supper you must say grace.

CLEVER DICK: Thanks for the grub, God.

MOTHER: That wasn't a very nice grace, Dick.

CLEVER DICK: It doesn't look like a very nice supper.

MOTHER: Did you know that most accidents happen in the kitchen?

CLEVER DICK: Yes – I have to eat them!

MOTHER: Did you thank Mrs Jones for inviting you to the party?

CLEVER DICK: No – the boy before me thanked her and Mrs Jones said 'Don't mention it', so I didn't.

MOTHER: Wash your hands, your piano teacher will soon be here.

CLEVER DICK: Don't worry, I'll only play on the black notes!

MOTHER: Have you changed the goldfish's water?

CLEVER DICK: No, he hasn't drunk what I gave him yesterday yet.

MOTHER: The florist has two children.
CLEVER DICK: I know. One's a budding genius and the other is a blooming idiot!

MOTHER: Why do you eat everything with your knife?
CLEVER DICK: My fork leaks!

MOTHER: Eggs are going up again.
CLEVER DICK: The chickens must have lost all sense of direction.

MOTHER: Why have you been sent home from school?
CLEVER DICK: Because John Jones was smoking.
MOTHER: But if he was smoking why have they sent you home?
CLEVER DICK: It was me that set him alight.

CLEVER DICK DAUGHTER: Mummy, Mummy, Jack has broken my doll!
MOTHER: How did he do that?
CLEVER DICK DAUGHTER: I hit him over the head with it.

MOTHER: What will you do when you're as big as your father?
CLEVER DICK: Go on a diet.

MOTHER: Have you put the cat out, darling?
CLEVER DICK: I think I must have. I just trod on his tail.

FRIEND: Do you like your mother?
CLEVER DICK: I can't complain — I don't dare!

FRIEND: Does your mother lie about her age?
CLEVER DICK: Not really. She says she's as old as my dad, then lies about his age!

MOTHER: Do you think it will rain today?
CLEVER DICK: It all depends on the weather.

FRIEND: My mother is an authority on Ancient Greece.
CLEVER DICK: You mean she never cleans the oven?

CLEVER DICK: I think my mother is too efficient.
FRIEND: What do you mean?
CLEVER DICK: Every time she goes on a two week diet, she finishes it in three days!

MOTHER: Your cap is on the wrong way, Dick.
CLEVER DICK: How do you know which way I'm going?

MOTHER: Did you put the cat out?
CLEVER DICK: Why? Is it on fire?

MOTHER: Dick, stop poking the baby.
CLEVER DICK: I'm not poking him, Mum, I'm counting his measles.

MOTHER: How did you get your hands so dirty?
CLEVER DICK: Washing my face.

MOTHER: Why did you hit your brother with a chair?
CLEVER DICK: I couldn't lift the table.

MOTHER: What do you think would go well with my new hat, dear?
CLEVER DICK: A blackout!

FRIEND: Is your mother hard to please?
CLEVER DICK: I don't know – I never tried.

MOTHER: When you yawn, put your hand in front of your mouth.
CLEVER DICK: What? And get bitten?

MOTHER: Darling, do you want to hear something awful?
CLEVER DICK: No, please, don't sing!

Clever Dick and Dad

CLEVER DICK: Dad, will you do my maths homework for me?
FATHER: Oh no, it wouldn't be right.
CLEVER DICK: Maybe, but at least you could try.

FATHER: What did you study at school today?
CLEVER DICK: Lots of things, but mostly gozinta.
FATHER: Gozinta? What's that, a foreign language?
CLEVER DICK: No, Dad, you know – three goes into six, five goes into ten . . .

FATHER: Did you learn anything today?
CLEVER DICK: Yes, but it wasn't enough. I have to go back again tomorrow.

FATHER: How do you like school?
CLEVER DICK: Closed.

CLEVER DICK: I got a bad school report because I got zero in one subject.
FATHER: Just one subject? What was it?
CLEVER DICK: Attendance.

FATHER: Son, I want you to have something that I never had when I was at school.
CLEVER DICK: What's that? Good marks?

FATHER: How were the questions in your exams at school today?
CLEVER DICK: Oh, the questions were easy – it was the answers that I had a bit of a problem with.

FATHER: What does the weather look like today?
CLEVER DICK: Can't tell – it's too foggy.

CLEVER DICK: Do you have a good memory for faces?
FATHER: Yes, why?
CLEVER DICK: I've just broken your shaving mirror!

CLEVER DICK SAYS: My Dad is so old, when he was at school history was called current events.

FRIEND: Does your mother have an automatic dishwasher?

CLEVER DICK: Yes — my father!

FRIEND: My father helps the church a great deal.

CLEVER DICK: So I understand. He never goes inside it!

CLEVER DICK SAYS: My dad wants to work badly — and he usually does!

FRIEND: Your dad claims to be around thirty.

CLEVER DICK: Yes, but he's been around it a few times.

FATHER: I hope you're not talking in class any more?

CLEVER DICK: Not any more, just about the same amount!

FRIEND: My father took an aptitude test, to find out what he was best suited for.

CLEVER DICK: Don't tell me — they discovered he was best suited for retirement!

FRIEND: Dad keeps saying Mum is very dear to him.

CLEVER DICK: He means she's costing him a fortune!

FATHER: The first thing you should do with a garden is turn it over.

CLEVER DICK: If I were you, I'd turn it over to someone who knows what they're doing!

FRIEND: My dad has his ups and downs.
CLEVER DICK: Does he? Mine just goes around in circles.

FATHER: Who gave you that black eye?
CLEVER DICK: Nobody gave it to me, I had to fight for it!

FRIEND: My mum wanted a man she could lean on.
CLEVER DICK: My mum did better than that. She got a man she could walk on!

FATHER: There's an energy crisis in our office.
CLEVER DICK: You mean your boss is expecting you to show some!

MOTHER: I want to give your father something striking and up-to-date for Christmas. Any ideas?
CLEVER DICK: A quartz alarm clock?

FATHER: You keep playing that guitar out of tune.
CLEVER DICK: It's not my fault. The electricity is flat!

CLEVER DICK: My father can't bear to see mum digging the garden.
FATHER: So what does he do about it?
CLEVER DICK: He draws the curtains.

FRIEND: Has your father ever raised his hand to you?
CLEVER DICK: Only in self-defence!

FRIEND: My father says there's no authority in the home.

CLEVER DICK: My father doesn't feel that way. He knows that whatever I say, goes!

FATHER: Plants grow faster if you talk to them.

CLEVER DICK: But I don't know how to speak geranium!

FATHER: Why don't you play with the boy next door any more?

CLEVER DICK: Would *you* play with cheats?

FATHER: Of course not.

CLEVER DICK: Neither will he.

CLEVER DICK SAYS: Every time my dad's car passes a scrap yard it gets homesick!

CLEVER DICK SAYS: My dad's car is for three people. One drives and two push!

FATHER: Why did you put a frog in your sister's bed?

CLEVER DICK: I couldn't find a dead mouse.

FRIEND: What is your father getting for Christmas?

CLEVER DICK: Fat and bald.

FATHER: So you failed the history exam?

CLEVER DICK: Yes, they kept asking questions about things that happened before I was born.

FATHER: You don't seem to realize which side your bread is buttered on.

CLEVER DICK: What does it matter? I eat both sides.

FATHER: No woman ever made a fool of me.

CLEVER DICK: Who did then?

FATHER: My doctor told me I can't play golf.

CLEVER DICK: So he's played with you, too, has he?

FATHER ON GOLF COURSE: Do you like my game?

CLEVER DICK: Not bad, but I still prefer golf!

Clever Dick and Sisters

CLEVER DICK: My sister must be twenty-nine years old.

FRIEND: How do you make that out?

CLEVER DICK: I counted the rings under her eyes.

CLEVER DICK: My sister's got musical feet.

FRIEND: How's that?

CLEVER DICK: They're both flat.

SISTER: I spend hours in front of a mirror admiring my beauty. Do you think it's vanity?

CLEVER DICK: No, a vivid imagination.

SISTER: Surely you must agree I sing with feeling?

CLEVER DICK: If you had any feeling you wouldn't sing.

CLEVER DICK SAYS: My sister's so fat that when she stands in the sun she casts two shadows.

SISTER: When I die I'm going to leave my brain to medical research.

CLEVER DICK: That's good. Every little bit helps.

38

SISTER: Do you think I should let my hair grow?
CLEVER DICK: Yes, right over your face.

SISTER: Did your music teacher really say my voice was heavenly?
CLEVER DICK: Not exactly – she said it was like nothing on earth.

SISTER (*Looking up from article about death statistics*): Do you know that every time I breathe a man dies?
CLEVER DICK: Very interesting. Have you tried toothpaste?

SISTER: Now look me straight in the face.
CLEVER DICK: I've got my own problems.

CLEVER DICK: Want to lose ten pounds of ugly fat?
SISTER: I'd love to.
CLEVER DICK: Cut off your head.

CLEVER DICK: My sister sings a lot for charity.
FRIEND: Does she?
CLEVER DICK: She has to. Nobody will pay her.

FRIEND: My sister has a soft heart.
CLEVER DICK: And a head to match.

SISTER: I wish I had a penny for every boy that has asked me out.
CLEVER DICK: At least you'd be able to go to the toilet, if nothing else.

SISTER: I bought this dress for a very low price.
CLEVER DICK: You mean for a ridiculous figure!

SISTER: Did you know that a man is knocked down by a car every thirty minutes?
CLEVER DICK: He must be getting awfully tired of it.

SISTER: Did you know that a woman gives birth to a baby every two minutes?
CLEVER DICK: She must be in the Guinness Book of Records.

FRIEND: Your sister's spoiled, isn't she?
CLEVER DICK: No, it's just the perfume she wears.

SISTER: I've just returned from the beauty parlour.
CLEVER DICK: Pity it was closed.

SISTER: Do you like my new hairstyle?
CLEVER DICK: In as much as it covers half your face, yes.

CLEVER DICK: There's a terrible, ugly thing on your shoulders.
SISTER: Help! What is it?
CLEVER DICK: Your head.

MOTHER: Your sister's a real treasure.
CLEVER DICK: I wish she was buried treasure.

FRIEND: How is your headache, Dick?
CLEVER DICK: Out at the disco with her boyfriend.

CLEVER DICK: That's a nice dress you're wearing.
SISTER: Thank you.
CLEVER DICK: I wonder if that style will ever come back?

FRIEND: My sister always wears a dress with a square neck.
CLEVER DICK: To go with her head.

CLEVER DICK SAYS: My sister has worn that dress so often, it's been in fashion six times!

FRIEND: My sister just bought a reversible coat.
CLEVER DICK: What she really needs is a reversible face.

SISTER: I'm putting on too much weight. What shall I do?
CLEVER DICK: Push yourself away from the table three times a day.

CLEVER DICK SAYS: The only time my sister's face gets washed is when she cries.

FRIEND: There's real beauty in my sister's face.
CLEVER DICK: If you can read between the lines.

FRIEND: I think my sister's face will be her fortune.
CLEVER DICK: Then she'll never have to pay income tax, that's for sure!

FRIEND: My sister has such a pretty chin.
CLEVER DICK: Too bad she added two more.

CLEVER DICK TO SISTER: Would you mind telling me what's on your mind — if you'll excuse the exaggeration.

CLEVER DICK: There's only one thing wrong with your face.

SISTER: What's that?

CLEVER DICK: It sticks out of your dress.

FRIEND: My sister always keeps her mirrors clean.

CLEVER DICK: Who wants to see dusty wrinkles?

CLEVER DICK SAYS: The longest I've known anything stay in her head is an hour – and that was a cold.

FRIEND: My sister has a face like a saint.

CLEVER DICK: Yeah, a St Bernard.

FRIEND: They say my sister has a promising voice.

CLEVER DICK: Perhaps she'll take notice and promise to stop singing.

FRIEND: My sister's going to have a coming out party.

CLEVER DICK: With her face, they'll probably make her go back in again.

FRIEND: I hear your sister doesn't care for a man's company?

CLEVER DICK: Not unless he owns it.

CLEVER DICK SAYS: The only way my sister can get some colour in her face is to stick out her tongue!

SISTER: I've decided to let my hair grow.
CLEVER DICK: How can you stop it?

CLEVER DICK: I like your dress.
SISTER: Thank you.
CLEVER DICK: But aren't you a little bit early for Halloween?

FRIEND: Does your sister like housework?
CLEVER DICK: She likes to do nothing better.

SISTER: Do you think I'll lose my looks as I get older?
CLEVER DICK: If you're lucky.

SISTER: I've changed my mind.
CLEVER DICK: Oh good – does it work better than the old one?

CLEVER DICK: I think my sister should have been born in the Dark Ages.
FRIEND: Why's that?
CLEVER DICK: She looks terrible in a bright light.

MOTHER: Did you notice how your sister's voice filled the hall at the school concert?
CLEVER DICK: Yes. I also noticed that a lot of people left to make room for it.

FRIEND: How's your sister getting on with her diet?
CLEVER DICK: Great – she almost disappeared!

FRIEND: We should take your sister at face value.

CLEVER DICK: With a face like hers, that's not worth much!

SISTER: Shall I put the kettle on?

CLEVER DICK: Don't bother, I prefer the dress you're already wearing!

SISTER: Don't I look lovely today?

CLEVER DICK: Yes, it's a real treat for people to see you. After all, it costs money to get into a freak show!

SISTER: What's the meaning of 'opaque'?

CLEVER DICK: Something that's too thick for light to pass through . . . your skull, for example!

SISTER: They say that two heads are better than one.

CLEVER DICK: In your case, none is better than one!

CLEVER DICK SAYS: My sister is like the jungle — dense!

FRIEND: My sister has a very sympathetic face.

CLEVER DICK: Yes, it has everyone's sympathy.

FRIEND: Why do you say that my sister is stupid?

CLEVER DICK: She told me she's working on a new invention: colour radio!

CLEVER DICK SAYS: Music has a terrible effect on my sister. It makes her sing!

FRIEND: The dresses my sister wears never go out of fashion.
CLEVER DICK: No, they look just as ridiculous year after year.

SISTER: Don't you think I have a perfect shape?
CLEVER DICK: Yes, perfectly round.

SISTER: They say that ignorance is bliss.
CLEVER DICK: Then you must be the happiest girl in the world!

SISTER: Do you think I look bad?
CLEVER DICK: You could look worse – if I had better eyesight.

SISTER: Men say I'm one in a million.
CLEVER DICK: Thank goodness!

FRIEND: Your sister seems very shy.
CLEVER DICK: I'll say. She even covers the bird cage when she takes her clothes off.

CLEVER DICK: Your sister should only go out on Halloween.
FRIEND: Why's that?
CLEVER DICK: It's the only time she can pass as normal.

FRIEND: My sister's not really bad looking.
CLEVER DICK: Apart from the little blemish between her ears – her face!

46

SISTER: Do you think I have a big mouth?
CLEVER DICK: Let's put it this way, you're the only person I know who can eat bananas sideways.

FRIEND: Do you think my sister has a big mouth?

CLEVER DICK: It's so big she can sing a duet all by herself.

CLEVER DICK SAYS: My sister's mouth is so big, when she yawns you can't see her ears!

SISTER: This sweater doesn't do much for me.

CLEVER DICK: The way you look in it, the wool looked better on the sheep!

SISTER: I'm really watching my weight.

CLEVER DICK: You mean, watching it go up!

CLEVER DICK: My sister has a waterproof voice.

FRIEND: What do you mean?

CLEVER DICK: It can't be drowned out.

CLEVER DICK: My sister talks like a photocopy machine.

FRIEND: What do you mean?

CLEVER DICK: She keeps repeating herself!

FRIEND: I hear that your two sisters stick together?

CLEVER DICK: If you took a bath as infrequently as they do, you'd be a bit sticky too!

SISTER: I might look quite heavy, but I'm a light eater.

CLEVER DICK: Yeah, as soon as it's light you start eating!

SISTER: I eat like a bird.
CLEVER DICK: Yeah, a vulture!

FRIEND: My sister once had a million-dollar figure.
CLEVER DICK: Pity inflation set in.

CLEVER DICK SAYS: Boys don't call my sister attractive, and they don't call her plain. They just don't call her.

CLEVER DICK: The Noise Abatement Society should send my sister a button.
FRIEND: What for?
CLEVER DICK: Her lip.

SISTER: Do you think success has gone to my head?
CLEVER DICK: Well it's certainly gone to your mouth!

SISTER: Do you think I'm puny-looking?
CLEVER DICK: No, it's just that if you ever get married, they won't throw confetti, they'll throw vitamin pills!

CLEVER DICK: I wish you'd sing only Christmas carols.
SISTER: Why?
CLEVER DICK: Because then I'd only have to listen to you once a year!

SISTER: Do you think I look like Helen Green?
CLEVER DICK: You look even worse in red!

FRIEND: My sister is a naturally talented 'cello player.

CLEVER DICK: I can tell that by her bow legs!

SISTER: What do you think of my singing?
CLEVER DICK: It reminds me that dad's car
  needs a tune-up!

Clever Dick and Brothers

FRIEND: My brother flies off the handle a lot.
CLEVER DICK: No wonder. He has a screw loose!

FRIEND: My brother is girl crazy.
CLEVER DICK: Yes, girls won't go out with him,
  and that's why he's crazy!

CLEVER DICK: My brother's like a summer cold.
FRIEND: What do you mean?
CLEVER DICK: You can't get rid of him!

BROTHER: Everybody ought to help clean up the
  environment.
CLEVER DICK: I agree. You could start with
  your room.

CLEVER DICK: My brother took ten years to
  finish university. He's a DD.
FRIEND: A Doctor of Divinity?
CLEVER DICK: No, a dum-dum!

CLEVER DICK: Is it true the human race springs
  from dust?
FRIEND: So they say.
CLEVER DICK: Well, under my brother's bed is
  the birth of a nation!

CLEVER DICK SAYS: Some kids train to be
  doctors or engineers when they grow up. My
  brother's training to be a swamp!

FRIEND: Do you know anybody who's been on
  the telly?
CLEVER DICK: My little brother did once, but he
  can use a potty now.

FRIEND: Is your brother a bookworm?
CLEVER DICK: No, just an ordinary one.

BOY: Mummy, am I descended from monkeys?
CLEVER DICK MOTHER: I really don't know. I've
  never met your father's family.

CLEVER DICK: My brother was born upside down.
FRIEND: How's that?
CLEVER DICK: His nose runs and his feet smell.

BROTHER: Can you lend me 10p – I want to telephone a friend.
CLEVER DICK: Here's 20p – ring them both.

FRIEND: What are you giving your brother for Christmas?
CLEVER DICK: I'm not sure yet. I gave him chickenpox last year.

FRIEND: Why is your brother so small?
CLEVER DICK: He's my half-brother.

FRIEND: I hear your brother went to a mind-reader yesterday. What happened?
CLEVER DICK: She gave him his money back.

CLEVER DICK: I cured my little brother of biting his nails.
FRIEND: How?
CLEVER DICK: I knocked all his teeth out.

MOTHER: Why is your brother crying?
CLEVER DICK: Because I won't give him my piece of cake.
MOTHER: What about his own piece?
CLEVER DICK: He cried when I ate that too!

BROTHER: Guess what my brain X-ray showed?
CLEVER DICK: Nothing?

BROTHER: I want to fight air pollution.
CLEVER DICK: You could start by not breathing.

CLEVER DICK SAYS: My brother's so crooked, he has to screw his socks on!

CLEVER DICK SAYS: My brother bites his nails so much, his stomach needs a manicure!

FRIEND: Have you noticed the strange growth on my brother's neck?
CLEVER DICK: I thought that was his head!

FRIEND: I reckon my kid brother has a chip on his shoulder.
CLEVER DICK: It's probably from the wooden block on his neck!

FRIEND: Everyone in our family is hoping my brother will get ahead.
CLEVER DICK: Yes, he looks a bit odd with nothing on top of his neck.

FRIEND: My brother often has something on his mind.
CLEVER DICK: Only when he wears a hat.

CLEVER DICK SAYS: When my brother was promoted from nursery school he was so excited he cut himself shaving!

FRIEND: Do you think my brother is ugly?
CLEVER DICK: Ugly? He probably has to sneak up on the mirror to shave.

54

BROTHER: Do you think I have big ears?

CLEVER DICK: Big? Why, you'll be able to swat flies with them!

BROTHER: I've been staying awake at night trying to work out how to succeed.
CLEVER DICK: You'd be better off staying awake during the day.

CLEVER DICK TO BROTHER: You look much better without my glasses!

CLEVER DICK TO BROTHER: When you were born, the doctor took one look at you and slapped Mum's face!

FRIEND: It's a pity about my brother's cross-eyes.
CLEVER DICK: Yes, but at least he can watch a tennis match without moving his head!

BROTHER: Is it true that carrots improve your sight?
CLEVER DICK: Have you ever seen a rabbit with glasses?

CLEVER DICK SAYS: My brother's such an idiot he put a bucket under a gas leak.

CLEVER DICK SAYS: I won't say my brother's hopeless at school, but he has to cheat to come last.

CLEVER DICK: My brother is so clumsy that if he fell down, he'd probably miss the floor.

BROTHER: Do you like my camel coat?
CLEVER DICK: No, it looks as if the camel's still inside it.

CLEVER DICK: That suit fits you like a glove.

BROTHER: I'm glad you like it.

CLEVER DICK: I don't. It sticks out in five places.

FRIEND: I just got this little puppy for my brother.

CLEVER DICK: Gosh! Whoever did you find to make a swap like that?

BROTHER: I have a leaning towards blondes.

CLEVER DICK: Pity they keep pushing you back.

FRIEND: My brother's very dependable.

CLEVER DICK: Sure. You can always depend on him to do the wrong thing!

CLEVER DICK SAYS: Any girl who goes out with my brother must appreciate the simpler things in life!

FRIEND: My brother has become very stupid.

CLEVER DICK: He must have been practising — you can't be that good at it by accident!

FRIEND: Your brother would never hit someone when they were down.

CLEVER DICK: No, he kicks them instead!

CLEVER DICK: When my brother goes to the zoo he needs two tickets.

FRIEND: Really? Why?

CLEVER DICK: One to get in and one to get out.

BROTHER: I do all my singing in the shower.
CLEVER DICK: Don't sing very often, do you?

BROTHER: When I sing people clap their hands.
CLEVER DICK: Yeah, over their ears.

BROTHER: I don't think I have many faults.
CLEVER DICK: No, but you certainly make the most of the ones you have.

CLEVER DICK TO BROTHER: It's obvious I can't get through to you – you have a sound-proof head.

FRIEND: Look at my new baby brother. The stork brought him.
CLEVER DICK: He looks more like a seagull dropped him.

BROTHER: Mum says that cleanliness is next to godliness.
CLEVER DICK: With you it's next to impossible!

Clever Dick and Brothers' Girlfriends

BROTHER: I think the mud packs my girlfriend wears improve her looks.
CLEVER DICK: For a few days, but then the mud falls off!

BROTHER: Pammy said she would only marry a guy who could take a joke.
CLEVER DICK: That's the only kind who would take her!

58

FRIEND: My brother's girlfriend returned all his letters.

CLEVER DICK: I bet she marked them '2nd Class Male'.

CLEVER DICK SAYS: My brother's girlfriend's family are such snobs. They even have monogrammed teabags!

FRIEND: Is your brother's girlfriend ugly?

CLEVER DICK: Ugly? Every time a mosquito bites her, it shuts its eyes!

BROTHER: Nobody can call my girlfriend a quitter.

CLEVER DICK: Of course not. She's been fired from every job she's had.

GIRL: My brother's girlfriend is the ugliest girl I ever saw.

CLEVER DICK: Present company excepted.

BROTHER: My girlfriend is as sweet as sugar.

CLEVER DICK: And twice as lumpy.

CLEVER DICK SAYS: My brother's girlfriend's ears are so big, she looks like a taxi with both doors open.

CLEVER DICK (*looking at brother's girlfriend*): I don't know. That must be a face — it has ears on it.

CLEVER DICK TO BROTHER: Is that your new girlfriend or just the old one painted over?

BROTHER: My girlfriend has a complexion like a peach.
CLEVER DICK: Yeah, yellow and fuzzy.

BROTHER: I don't know what to give my girlfriend. She doesn't smoke.
CLEVER DICK: Give her flowers. She smells.

FRIEND: I hear your brother's new girlfriend is an actress. Is she good looking?
CLEVER DICK: Well, I wouldn't say she's ugly, but she's got a perfect face for radio.

FRIEND: I think your brother's girlfriend is really good looking. She's got long blonde hair all down her back.
CLEVER DICK: Pity it doesn't grow on her head.

FRIEND: I've heard your brother's girlfriend has got big ears?
CLEVER DICK: I'll say. From the back she looks like the F.A. cup.

FRIEND: How good looking is your brother's new girlfriend?
CLEVER DICK: I won't exactly say she's ugly, but at Christmas the boys hang her up and kiss the mistletoe.

BROTHER: I wonder why my new girlfriend doesn't wear lipstick?
CLEVER DICK: She chats so much she can't keep her mouth still long enough to put it on.

BROTHER: My girlfriend looks a bit tired.

CLEVER DICK: You're not joking. I demanded to see her birth certificate to prove she's alive!

BROTHER: My girlfriend has gone to the beauty parlour.

CLEVER DICK: I didn't know they could perform miracles!

FRIEND: Is your brother's new girlfriend good looking?

CLEVER DICK: Let's put it this way: her facial features don't seem to know the importance of teamwork . . .

BROTHER: I'm going out with a girl who's different from all the other girls.

CLEVER DICK: You mean, she's the only girl in town who'll go out with you!

CLEVER DICK SAYS: My brother's girlfriend is so ugly she rents herself out for Halloween parties.

CLEVER DICK SAYS: My brother's girlfriend is so ugly she can walk the streets on Halloween without a mask.

CLEVER DICK TO BROTHER'S GIRL FRIEND: Is that your real face or are you still celebrating Halloween?

BROTHER: My girlfriend has a heart of gold.

CLEVER DICK: Yellow and hard.

BROTHER: I think my new girlfriend is like an angel fallen from the sky.
CLEVER DICK: Too bad she fell on her face.

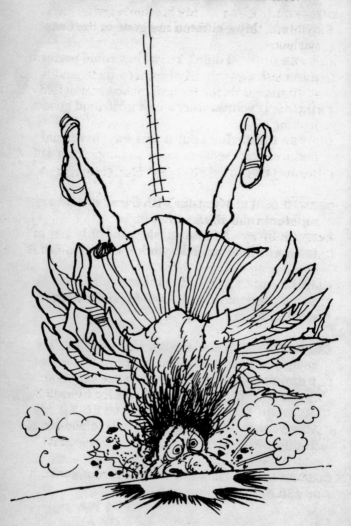

BROTHER: My new girlfriend has a big heart.
CLEVER DICK: And a stomach to match.

CLEVER DICK SAYS: My brother's girlfriend is so dumb, the only thing she ever read was an eye chart.

CLEVER DICK SAYS: My brother's girlfriend is so dumb, she'd look for a wishbone in a boiled egg.

Clever Dick and Sisters' Boyfriends

CLEVER DICK: My sister's boyfriend is not very popular in the office.
FRIEND: Why's that?
CLEVER DICK: The other workers complain that his snoring disturbs them.

CLEVER DICK SAYS: My sister's boyfriend is a real baboon to society.

FRIEND: I've often wondered why my sister's boyfriend never takes a shower.
CLEVER DICK: It's probably because the steam clouds the mirror so he can't admire himself!

CLEVER DICK: A photographer took a picture of my sister's boyfriend but never developed it.
FRIEND: Why not?
CLEVER DICK: He was afraid to be alone with it in a dark room!

FRIEND: My sister's boyfriend is a person who's going places.

CLEVER DICK: The sooner the better!

FRIEND: There's one good thing you can say for my sister's boyfriend: he puts in a good day's work.

CLEVER DICK: Yeah, but it takes him a month.

FRIEND: Is your sister's boyfriend really that lazy?

CLEVER DICK: Listen, he's so lazy he even sticks his nose out the window so the wind can blow it for him.

FRIEND: My sister's boyfriend holds people open-mouthed with his conversation.

CLEVER DICK: Of course — they can't stop yawning.

FRIEND: My sister's boyfriend is a man of rare gifts.

CLEVER DICK: You mean, he hasn't given one in years.

CLEVER DICK SAYS: The only thing my sister's boyfriend can do fast is get tired.

CLEVER DICK SAYS: There's only one job my sister's boyfriend would really like — tester in a mattress factory!

FRIEND: I'm told your sister's boyfriend buys her jewellery from a famous millionaire.

CLEVER DICK: True — Woolworth.

CLEVER DICK: Your sister's boyfriend's right eye must be fascinating.

FRIEND: Why?

CLEVER DICK: Because his left eye keeps looking at it!

FRIEND: My sister's boyfriend is very sincere.

CLEVER DICK: Really? I thought the only genuine thing about him is his false teeth.

SISTER: A few minutes with my boyfriend and I feel like jumping for joy.

CLEVER DICK: I feel like jumping off the roof!

SISTER: I tell you, he's not conceited.

CLEVER DICK: No, he just loves his good looks and personality.

CLEVER DICK: My sister's boyfriend's thoughts are written all over his face.

FRIEND: Really?

CLEVER DICK: Yes, he's always got a blank expression.

SISTER: Do you think my boyfriend is conceited?

CLEVER DICK: Who else has a mirror on the bathroom ceiling so he can watch himself gargle?

CLEVER DICK: When my sister's boyfriend is talking, I always think of an explosion in a coal mine.

FRIEND: Why?

CLEVER DICK: A lot of noise coming out of a big hole.

SISTER: Look what my boyfriend gave me for my birthday — a mink stole.
CLEVER DICK: I'm not sure it's mink, but I'm certain it's stole!

SISTER: I've lost my warm feelings for Sid.
CLEVER DICK: You'll soon get them back when he buys you a fur coat!

SISTER'S BOYFRIEND: My boss was sorry when I told him I was quitting next month.
CLEVER DICK: He was probably hoping it was this month.

SISTER: My boyfriend was cut out to be a genius.
CLEVER DICK: It's too bad nobody took the trouble to put the pieces together.

FRIEND: My sister's boyfriend took her for better or for worse.
CLEVER DICK: But he didn't mean *that* much worse!

FRIEND: My sister's boyfriend calls her baby face.
CLEVER DICK: Does he tell her she has a brain to match?

FRIEND: My sister's boyfriend is very well groomed.
CLEVER DICK: Yes, he always takes a shower once a month whether he thinks he needs it or not.

SISTER: My boyfriend wanted to be a mechanic badly.

CLEVER DICK: Well he's realized his ambition. He's a bad mechanic.

FRIEND: My sister's boyfriend is welcome in the best homes.

CLEVER DICK: Of course he is — he's a plumber!

CLEVER DICK SAYS: It's been so long since my sister's boyfriend stood upright, his shadow is crooked!

FRIEND: Is it true that your sister's boyfriend is a miracle worker?

CLEVER DICK: That's right. It's a miracle when he works!

CLEVER DICK SAYS: My sister's boyfriend would have difficulty counting to twenty if he hadn't learnt how to take off his shoes.

CLEVER DICK: Even my sister's boyfriend's nose is lazy.

FRIEND: What do you mean?

CLEVER DICK: It won't even run when he has a cold.

FRIEND: My sister's boyfriend speaks Spanish like a native.

CLEVER DICK: Yeah, like a native Bulgarian.

FRIEND: My sister's boyfriend can tear a telephone book in half.

CLEVER DICK: *My* sister's boyfriend would have trouble with a wet Kleenex.

FRIEND: My sister's boyfriend has got a photographic mind.

CLEVER DICK: Too bad it never developed.

CLEVER DICK TO SISTER'S BOYFRIEND: Is that your nose or are you eating a banana?

FRIEND: My sister's boyfriend is a man of rare intelligence.
CLEVER DICK: So rare it seldom sees the light of day.

CLEVER DICK: My sister's boyfriend has been fired for working eight hours and sleeping eight hours.
FRIEND: Sounds normal enough – why was he fired?
CLEVER DICK: They were the same eight hours.

FRIEND: I've heard your sister's boyfriend is a very economical person?
CLEVER DICK: Well, he likes to save on soap and water.
FRIEND: Your sister's boyfriend isn't so bad looking. He does have even teeth.

CLEVER DICK: True. It's the odd ones that are missing.

CLEVER DICK TO SISTER'S BOYFRIEND: Is that your face or are you wearing your hair back to front?

SISTER: My boyfriend is very polite.
CLEVER DICK: Yes, he always takes his shoes off before he puts his feet on the table.

CLEVER DICK SAYS: Big noses run in my sister's boyfriend's family . . .

SISTER: We bumped into some old friends last week.
CLEVER DICK: Your boyfriend was driving again, was he?

SISTER: My boyfriend's written a novel to be published after he's dead.
CLEVER DICK: I can't wait to read it.

CLEVER DICK: I'm glad you don't have a dual personality.
SISTER'S BOYFRIEND: Why?
CLEVER DICK: The one you have is bad enough!

CLEVER DICK: It's hard for my sister's boyfriend to eat.
FRIEND: Why?
CLEVER DICK: He hates to stop talking!

FRIEND: My sister's boyfriend loves nature.
CLEVER DICK: That's good of him, considering what nature did to him!

CLEVER DICK: My sister's boyfriend told her he'd lost all his money.
FRIEND: What did she say?
CLEVER DICK: I'll miss you, darling.

Clever Dick and Grandad

FRIEND: My grandad is scared of flying.
CLEVER DICK: Scared? My grandad is so terrified he feels sick just licking an airmail stamp!

FRIEND: Do you think my grandad looks old?
CLEVER DICK: Old? He has so many wrinkles on his forehead, he has to screw on his hat!

CLEVER DICK: I was going to buy you some handkerchiefs for your birthday, Grandad.
GRANDAD: That was very kind of you.
CLEVER DICK: Trouble was, I couldn't find any big enough for your nose.

FRIEND: When my grandfather was born, they passed out cigars. When my father was born, they passed out cigarettes.
CLEVER DICK: And when you were born, they passed out.

CLEVER DICK SAYS: According to our doctor, grandad has too little blood in his alcohol system.

FRIEND: My grandad goes to the dentist once a year.
CLEVER DICK: Mine goes twice a year — once for each tooth!

FRIEND: My grandad get his exercise by walking to the pub.
CLEVER DICK: Mine gets his exercise watching horror movies on the video. They make his flesh creep!

FRIEND: What makes you say your grandad is short-sighted?
CLEVER DICK: He once picked up a snake to kill a stick!

GRANDAD: I have a Roman nose.
CLEVER DICK: Yes, it roams all over your face.

FRIEND: My grandparents are real swingers.
CLEVER DICK: From tree to tree?

CLEVER DICK SAYS: My grandad has become so bald, you can't look at him in a bright light without sunglasses.

Clever Dick and Grandma

GRANDMA BENT OVER THE PRAM: Oooo, you sweet little thing. I could eat you.
CLEVER DICK: Like heck you could. You haven't got any teeth.

CLEVER DICK: These are grandma's ashes.
FRIEND: Oh, did the poor old lady pass away?
CLEVER DICK: No. She's just too lazy to get up and fetch an ashtray.

FRIEND: What's your grandmother like?
CLEVER DICK: Well, I wouldn't exactly say she was mean, but she keeps a fork in the sugar bowl.

CLEVER DICK: Grandmother! Use the bottle opener – you'll ruin your gums!

CLEVER DICK: When grandma was little, people used to call her the wonder girl.
FRIEND: Why was that?
CLEVER DICK: They used to look at her and wonder.

CLEVER DICK SAYS: Grandma has the craziest hobby: all day long she sits in the corner and collects dust.

CLEVER DICK TO GRANDMA AT FUNERAL: How old are you, Grandma?

GRANDMA: Ninety-seven.

CLEVER DICK: Hardly worth going home, is it?

GRANDMA: Last night's dinner was awful. I hope you're going to give me something I can get my teeth into tonight.

CLEVER DICK: We certainly are. Here's a glass of water.

CLEVER DICK: Grandma, can you impersonate a frog?

GRANDMA: No. Why do you ask?

CLEVER DICK: 'Cos Mum says we'll get £30,000 when you croak.

DOCTOR: The pain in your leg is caused by old age.

CLEVER DICK GRANDMA: But doctor, my other leg is the same age and it doesn't hurt!

Clever Dick and Aunts and Uncles

FRIEND: They say that your aunt's stories always have a happy ending.

CLEVER DICK: Well, everybody's always happy when they end!

FRIEND: Is it true that your aunt is a fast talker?

CLEVER DICK: Fast talker? She can speak 150 words a minute, with gusts of up to 200!

AUNT: Your uncle is a man of few words.

CLEVER DICK: Too bad he keeps repeating them!

CLEVER DICK SAYS: My uncle's so bald, his head keeps slipping off the pillow at night!

CLEVER DICK: Before my aunt got married, her chin was her best feature.

FRIEND: And now?

CLEVER DICK: Now it's a double feature!

CLEVER DICK: You can always pick my uncle out.

FRIEND: How?

CLEVER DICK: If you see two people talking and one looks bored stiff, he's the other one.

CLEVER DICK SAYS: If my aunt's nose was turned up any more, she'd blow off her hat every time she sneezed.

FRIEND: I hear the Queen spoke to your aunt for a few seconds?

CLEVER DICK: Yes, but it takes her a few hours to describe it.

CLEVER DICK SAYS: Anything my aunt hears goes in one ear and out through the telephone.

CLEVER DICK SAYS: When there's nothing more to be said on a subject you can be sure my aunt will still be saying it!

FRIEND: My uncle's been trying to drown his troubles for years.

CLEVER DICK: So why hasn't he managed it? Your aunt too good a swimmer?

CLEVER DICK SAYS: My uncle is the only person I know who brightens a room when he goes out.

CLEVER DICK SAYS: My uncle's so boring he couldn't even entertain a doubt.

FRIEND: Is your uncle a lazy gardener?
CLEVER DICK: Lazy? The only thing I've ever seen him grow is tired.

CLEVER DICK SAYS: My uncle's such an old misery that even his shadow keeps as far away as it can.

CLEVER DICK TO AUNT: I see you're starting to show your true colours. Isn't it time you had another rinse?

FRIEND: My aunt has got everything a man could wish for.
CLEVER DICK: Including a moustache and rippling muscles.

CLEVER DICK SAYS: The only thing that makes my aunt look reasonable is distance!

FRIEND: My aunt had a face lift but it didn't work.
CLEVER DICK: Why not, did the crane break?

FRIEND: My uncle is good for people's health.
CLEVER DICK: You mean, when they see him coming they take a long walk!

FRIEND: I hear your aunt always has to have the last word.
CLEVER DICK: That wouldn't be so bad if she ever reached it . . .

CLEVER DICK SAYS: My aunt doesn't hold a conversation, she strangles it!

FRIEND: Your uncle is really bald.
CLEVER DICK: He thinks of himself as simply having a wide parting!

FRIEND: I hear your aunt once appeared in a beauty contest and got several offers.
CLEVER DICK: Yes, from plastic surgeons!

AUNT: Your uncle is a bit dull until you get to know him.
CLEVER DICK: After that he's a real bore!

CLEVER DICK SAYS: My uncle's a bit boring, but he does have occasional flashes of silence.

CLEVER DICK SAYS: My aunt is so fussy she won't even eat a hot dog unless it's been certified by the Kennel Club!

UNCLE: Your poor aunt can't see any further than the nose on her face.
CLEVER DICK: With a nose like hers, that's quite a distance.

AUNT: Do you like my dress? It's over a hundred years old.
CLEVER DICK: Did you make it yourself?

FRIEND: They say your aunt is rather cold-blooded.
CLEVER DICK: Cold-blooded? If a mosquito bit her it would die of frost-bite!

2 Clever Dick at School

TEACHER: Don't whistle while you're studying.
CLEVER DICK: I'm not studying – just
whistling.

TEACHER: Why are you so late in school?
CLEVER DICK: I had to say goodbye to my pets.
TEACHER: But you're two hours late.
CLEVER DICK: I've got an ant farm!

TEACHER: I'd like to go one whole day without
having to tell you off.
CLEVER DICK: Go ahead, you have my
permission.

TEACHER: I wish you'd pay a little attention.
CLEVER DICK: I'm paying as little as I can!

TEACHER: I'm expelling you from class!
CLEVER DICK: No you're not – I resign!

TEACHER: You should have been here at nine
o'clock!
CLEVER DICK: Why, what happened?

TEACHER: What's the death rate in our town?
CLEVER DICK: Same as any other place – one
death per person.

TEACHER: Did you have trouble with your French in France?
CLEVER DICK: No, but the French did.

CLEVER DICK: I'm glad I wasn't born in France.
TEACHER: Why's that?
CLEVER DICK: I can't speak a word of French.

TEACHER: Were you in France for your holidays?
CLEVER DICK: I don't know, my dad bought the tickets.

FRIEND: Why do you call your teacher 'Treasure'?
CLEVER DICK: Because I wonder where she was dug up!

TEACHER: Why are you so late?
CLEVER DICK: I'm sorry, but I overslept.
TEACHER: Do you mean to say that you sleep at home as well?

TEACHER: You missed school yesterday, didn't you?
CLEVER DICK: Yes, sir – next time I'll try to improve my aim.

TEACHER: You missed school yesterday, didn't you?
CLEVER DICK: No, not a bit.

TEACHER: What did I say I'd do if I caught you eating in class again?
CLEVER DICK: That's funny – I can't remember either.

TEACHER: How many seasons are there?
CLEVER DICK: Two, sir – football and cricket.

CAREERS MASTER: What will you be when you leave school?

CLEVER DICK: Happy, sir.

HEADMASTER: This is the fifth time this week that you've been sent to me for punishment. What have you got to say for yourself?

CLEVER DICK: Thank goodness it's Friday.

CLEVER DICK: Does the school bus run on time?

TEACHER: Usually, yes.

CLEVER DICK: That's funny, I thought it ran on petrol.

HEADMASTER ON CLEVER DICK'S FIRST DAY: And what might your name be?

CLEVER DICK: It might be Sebastian – but it isn't.

HEADMASTER: What's your name, boy?

CLEVER DICK: Dick.

HEADMASTER: You're supposed to say 'sir'.

CLEVER DICK: All right, *Sir* Dick.

TEACHER: Why weren't you in school yesterday?

CLEVER DICK: I had a bad tooth.

TEACHER: Is it better now?

CLEVER DICK: I don't know – I left it with the dentist.

TEACHER: Is your cough any better this morning?

CLEVER DICK: It should be, I've been practising all night.

TEACHER: Why are you scratching yourself?
CLEVER DICK: Because no one else knows where I itch.

TEACHER: Why are you chewing gum in my class?
CLEVER DICK: I couldn't get any toffees.

TEACHER TO NEW PUPILS: We start promptly at nine o'clock every morning.
CLEVER DICK: That's okay by me, but if I'm not here just start without me.

TEACHER TO NOISY CLASS: Order! Order!
CLEVER DICK: I'll have sausage, egg and chips, please.

TEACHER: Your hands are awfully dirty. What would you say if I came to school with hands as dirty as that?
CLEVER DICK: Nothing, sir – I'd be too polite to mention it.

TEACHER: What were you doing behind the bicycle sheds after school yesterday? I want an explanation – and I want the truth.
CLEVER DICK: Do you want them both?

TEACHER: If you keep getting things wrong, Dick, I don't see much of a future for you.
CLEVER DICK: That's all right, sir. When I leave school I want to be a weather forecaster.

TEACHER: Which month has twenty-eight days?
CLEVER DICK: They all do!

TEACHER: Why is it that you can never answer any of my questions?

CLEVER DICK: If I could, there would be no point in me coming to school.

TEACHER: What do you know about Good Friday?

CLEVER DICK: He did all the work for Robinson Crusoe.

TEACHER: Are you taking the bus home?

CLEVER DICK: No, my mother would only make me take it back again.

TEACHER: Now, if I saw a man beating a donkey and stopped him, what virtue would I be showing?

CLEVER DICK: Brotherly love?

TEACHER: Your writing seems to get worse instead of better.

CLEVER DICK: But if you could read my writing you'd notice my bad spelling.

CLEVER DICK: Would you punish a pupil for something they didn't do?

TEACHER: Of course not.

CLEVER DICK: Good. I haven't done my homework.

TEACHER: If a famous murderer was born in America, grew up in Australia, and then came to Britain and died, what would he be?

CLEVER DICK: Dead.

TEACHER: Where is your pencil?

CLEVER DICK: I ain't got one.

TEACHER: Not 'ain't' – 'haven't'. I *haven't* got a pencil, you *haven't* got a pencil, they *haven't* got pencils.

CLEVER DICK: Gosh! What happened to all the pencils?

TEACHER: Did your big brother help you with your homework, Dick?

CLEVER DICK: No, sir, he did it all himself.

TEACHER: How do you make a Venetian blind?

CLEVER DICK: Stick your finger in his eye.

TEACHER: How do you make a Maltese cross?

CLEVER DICK: Stamp on his foot.

TEACHER: Dick, what is the Order of the Bath?

CLEVER DICK: Mum, Dad, then me.

TEACHER: How do you make anti-freeze?

CLEVER DICK: Hide her thermal underwear.

TEACHER: What would happen if your brother had a brain transplant, Dick?

CLEVER DICK: The brain would reject him, sir.

TEACHER: Have you read the Bible?

CLEVER DICK: No, I'm waiting to see the film.

TEACHER: Now, now, you shouldn't fight, you should learn to give and take.

CLEVER DICK: I did, I gave him a black eye and I took his crisps.

TEACHER: Why are you jumping up and down?
CLEVER DICK: I took some medicine and forgot to shake the bottle.

TEACHER: Name the four seasons.
CLEVER DICK: Salt, pepper, vinegar and mustard.

TEACHER: If you found 50p in one pocket of your trousers and 70p in another, what would you have?
CLEVER DICK: Someone else's trousers!

TEACHER: Why were the Red Indians the first people in North America?
CLEVER DICK: Because they had reservations!

TEACHER: What do surgeons do with their mistakes?
CLEVER DICK: Bury them.

TEACHER: Don't you look in the mirror when you've washed your face?
CLEVER DICK: No, I look on the towel!

CLEVER DICK: I washed my budgie in detergent and it died.
TEACHER: You shouldn't have done that.
CLEVER DICK: It wasn't the detergent that killed it. It was the spin drier.

TEACHER: How can you tell if it's raining?
CLEVER DICK: Send your little sister outside and see if she comes in wet.

FRIEND: Our teacher can do bird imitations.
CLEVER DICK: I know. She watches me like a hawk.

TEACHER: You're pretty dirty, Dick.
CLEVER DICK: I'm even prettier clean.

TEACHER: Take your hands out of your pockets!
CLEVER DICK: I can't, sir, my belt has broken.

TEACHER: What has four legs and flies?
CLEVER DICK: A dead horse.

HEADMASTER: Are you chewing gum?
CLEVER DICK: No, sir – I'm John Brown.

TEACHER: Why didn't you wash your hands?
CLEVER DICK: What's the use, they'll only get dirty again.

TEACHER: You can't sleep in my class.
CLEVER DICK: But if you talked a little more quietly I could!

CLEVER DICK TO TEACHER AS HE HANDS IN HIS TEST PAPER: I think you'll find my answers are a good indication of your ability as a teacher.

CLEVER DICK: Some days I like my teacher.
MOTHER: When's that?
CLEVER DICK: When she's sick and has to stay home!

TEACHER: Do you ever lie?
CLEVER DICK: Let's just say my memory
   exaggerates!

CLEVER DICK SAYS: *Rip out this page and pin it
to your desk*

BEHIND THIS DESK
IS A PUPIL WHOSE

LATENT GENIUS,
IF UNLEASHED,
WOULD ROCK THE NATION...
WHOSE DYNAMIC ENERGY
WOULD OVERPOWER
ALL THOSE AROUND HIM...

... BETTER LET HIM
SLEEP !

CLEVER DICK: *Rip out this page and pin it to the school notice board.*

★ IN CASE OF FIRE ★

GATHER UP AS MANY
EXERCISE BOOKS AS POSSIBLE
AND RUN TOWARDS
THE FLAMES.

CLEVER DICK SAYS: *Cut out these great slogans and stick them on your exercise books!*

Help your headmaster — give yourself the cane.

You don't have to be crazy to come to this school — but it helps.

Save energy — learn slowly.

Our teacher is boss-eyed — he can't control his pupils.

Cut education costs — fire all the teachers.

Cut education costs — play truant!

I like going to school. I like coming home. It's the bit in between I don't like.

They call this a comprehensive school but I can't comprehend a thing.

80% of headmasters take *The Times*. The remaining 20% buy it.

Save our school — shoot the cook.

Our school meals are so tough you can't get your fork into the gravy.

I'd enjoy the school day more if it started later.

CLEVER DICK SAYS: *Here's how to send your teachers completely round the twist . . .*

. . . If you've answered a question and they still want to hear more, say:

'I know you believe you understand what you think I said, but I am not sure you realize that what you heard is not what I meant.'

SPORTS MASTER: Why don't you try the high jump?
CLEVER DICK: I'm scared of heights.

CLEVER DICK: You played a great game.
TEAM MATE: I thought I played rather badly.
CLEVER DICK: I meant you played a great game for the other side.

SPORTS MASTER: Who was the fastest runner in history?
CLEVER DICK: Adam — he was the first in the human race!

CLEVER DICK: If there's a referee in football and an umpire in cricket, what do you have in bowls?
SPORTS MASTER: I have no idea.
CLEVER DICK: Goldfish of course!

SPORTS MASTER: Why didn't you stop that ball?
CLEVER DICK GOALKEEPER: I thought the net would stop it.

CLEVER DICK SAYS: Our school cook is so bad she even burns cornflakes!

CLEVER DICK SAYS: Our school dinners are so cold that the potatoes always wear their jackets!

TEACHER: Dick, why are you the only child in class today?

CLEVER DICK: Because I was the only one who didn't have a school dinner yesterday.

GIRL: Where are you going?

CLEVER DICK: I've got a football match this afternoon and I'm in the school team.

GIRL: I bet it's exciting for you when you win.

CLEVER DICK: I don't know – I've only been in the team for two seasons.

CLEVER DICK: My new football boots hurt me.

SPORTS MASTER: I'm not surprised – you're wearing them on the wrong feet.

CLEVER DICK: I can't help it, These are the only feet I've got.

CLEVER DICK: What's this?

CANTEEN LADY: It's bean soup.

CLEVER DICK: I don't care what it's been. What is it now?

CLEVER DICK: Have you got any custard left?

CANTEEN LADY: Yes.

CLEVER DICK: Well you shouldn't have made so much then!

CLEVER DICK TO CANTEEN LADY: What's this on my plate – just in case I have to describe it to the school doctor?

CLEVER DICK: I bet we've got salad for lunch today.

CANTEEN LADY: That's right. How did you know?

CLEVER DICK: I couldn't smell anything burning.

CANTEEN LADY: Eat up your spinach, it'll put colour in your cheeks.

CLEVER DICK: Maybe, but who wants green cheeks?

MOTHER: What did you have for dinner at school today?

CLEVER DICK: A mixture of modern technology and past history.

MOTHER: What on earth was that?

CLEVER DICK: Micro-chips in ancient grease.

GIRL: Is it good manners to eat chickens with your fingers?

CLEVER DICK: No, you should eat your fingers separately.

CLEVER DICK: What's this?

CANTEEN LADY: Cottage pie.

CLEVER DICK: I thought so – I've just eaten part of the door.

CLEVER DICK: Could I have a horrible shrivelled up fried egg with hairs on it, some cold greasy chips, and some rock hard peas, please?

CANTEEN LADY: I don't serve food like that!

CLEVER DICK: Well, you did yesterday.

CLEVER DICK: I don't like the way you've made this pie.

CANTEEN LADY: What? I'll have you know I was making pies before you were born.

CLEVER DICK: I think this is one of them.

CANTEEN LADY: Do you want seconds?

CLEVER DICK: No, thank you – I'm too young to die.

CANTEEN LADY: Eat your cabbage, it's full of iron.

CLEVER DICK: So that's why it's so tough!

CLEVER DICK: May I have some fish?

CANTEEN LADY: With pleasure.

CLEVER DICK: No, with chips.

CANTEEN LADY: And after your main course what will you have to follow?

CLEVER DICK: If it's anything like yesterday's meal I'll probably have indigestion.

CLEVER DICK SAYS: Our school dinners are so bad even the dustbins have ulcers!

HEADMASTER IN ASSEMBLY: I'm sorry to have to tell you that school meals are going up again.

CLEVER DICK: They're difficult to keep down!

GIRL: Did you know there was an accident in the school canteen yesterday?

CLEVER DICK: Yes, I know – I had it for my lunch!

93

BOY: There isn't any steak and kidney in this steak and kidney pie.

CLEVER DICK: Of course not — you wouldn't expect a shepherd in a shepherd's pie, would you?

CLEVER DICK'S COMMENT ON IRISH STEW: Ah, the policeman's favourite meal — Irish stew in the name of the law.

CLEVER DICK'S COMMENT ON COTTAGE PIE: I know you're a perfectionist, but there was no need to put thatch on it.

CLEVER DICK'S COMMENT ON CURRY: Can I take this home in a curryer bag?

CLEVER DICK'S COMMENT ON TREACLE TART: Can I take a barrow load home with me? My dad wants to lay a new garden path.

CLEVER DICK'S COMMENT ON FISH FINGERS: What have you done with the thumbs?

CLEVER DICK'S COMMENT ON STEAK: I've heard of being burned at the stake, but this steak is really burned!

CLEVER DICK'S COMMENT ON SHEPHERD'S PIE: Is it made with real shepherds?

CLEVER DICK'S COMMENT ON DUMPLINGS: Can I take one home? I need a new cricket ball.

CLEVER DICK'S COMMENT ON FISH: It looks as though it's had its chips.

HEADMASTER: From today there will be no
more physical punishment in this school.
CLEVER DICK: I guess that means no more
school dinners!

DINNER MENUS : WHAT THEY SAY ... AND
WHAT THEY REALLY MEAN

What it says on the board	*What to ask for*
Plums and custard	Conkers in slime
Jam tart	Blood-soaked bandages
Rice with jam	Septic wound
Tapioca	Frog spawn
Semolina	Wallpaper paste
Spaghetti bolognaise	Worms in sewage
Sausages	UFOs (Unidentified Frying Objects)
Sausages and mash	Suspicion and trash
Steak and kidney	Snake and pygmy
Faggots	Maggot meatballs
Egg and chips	Eyeball and soggy fingers
Chocolate custard	Radioactive effluent

DELICIOUS INSULTS FOR THE DINNER LADY...

★ This fly looks extremely well-cooked.
★ Did you kill this cabbage yourself?
★ The sauce looks very artistic – just like
   paint.
★ Do you serve Rennies for dessert?
★ What kind of eggs are these – pterodactyl's?
★ May I have another plate for the maggots?
★ I know the fish fingers are dead, but there
   was no need to cremate them.

95

★ Are those sultanas, or do you keep rabbits under the counter?

★ Are these sesame seeds, or have you been picking your nose?

CLEVER DICK: Sir, how do you spell 'orrible?

ENGLISH TEACHER: Don't you mean horrible?

CLEVER DICK: No, sir. I've written the H already.

ENGLISH TEACHER: Name three collective nouns.

CLEVER DICK: Fly paper, waste paper basket, and vacuum cleaner.

ENGLISH TEACHER: What are you reading?

CLEVER DICK: I don't know.

ENGLISH TEACHER: But you were reading aloud.

CLEVER DICK: I know, but I wasn't listening.

ENGLISH TEACHER: Spell 'tiger'.

CLEVER DICK: T-i-g-e.

ENGLISH TEACHER: But what's at the end of it?

CLEVER DICK: A tail.

ENGLISH TEACHER: Your essay about cricket was rather short.

CLEVER DICK: Yes, sir. That's because rain stopped play.

ENGLISH TEACHER: You were supposed to write two pages about milk but you've only done one.

CLEVER DICK: It's condensed milk.

ENGLISH TEACHER: I hope you understand the importance of punctuation?

CLEVER DICK: Oh yes, sir – I always get to school on time.

ENGLISH TEACHER: You and Jones handed in exactly the same essay about a football match.

CLEVER DICK: Yes, sir, it was the same match.

ENGLISH TEACHER: Give me a sentence with the word 'centimetre' in it.

CLEVER DICK: Er . . . my aunt was coming home from the country and I was centimetre.

ENGLISH TEACHER: Take this sentence: 'Let the cow be taken to the field.' Now, what mood?

CLEVER DICK: The cow, sir?

ENGLISH TEACHER: How do you spell 'crocodile'?

CLEVER DICK: K-r-o-k-o-d-i-a-l.

ENGLISH TEACHER: The dictionary spells it c-r-o-c-o-d-i-l-e.

CLEVER DICK: You didn't ask me how the dictionary spelt it.

ENGLISH TEACHER: Say something beginning with 'I'

CLEVER DICK: I is . . .

ENGLISH TEACHER: No, you must say 'I am'.

CLEVER DICK: All right, I am the ninth letter of the alphabet.

ENGLISH TEACHER: Are you an avid reader?

CLEVER DICK: I don't know. I never read Avid.

ENGLISH TEACHER: Have you read Shakespeare?

CLEVER DICK: No, but I do have red pyjamas.

ENGLISH TEACHER: What did Juliet say when she met Romeo on the balcony?
CLEVER DICK: 'Couldn't you get seats in the stalls?'

ENGLISH TEACHER: How do you spell Mississippi?
CLEVER DICK: River or state?

GEOGRAPHY TEACHER: What sort of money do Eskimos use?
CLEVER DICK: Iced lolly!

GEOGRAPHY TEACHER: Dick, how can you prove that the world is round?
CLEVER DICK: I never said it was, sir.

GEOGRAPHY TEACHER: What is a Red Indian's wife called?
PUPIL: A squaw.
GEOGRAPHY TEACHER: That's right. And what are Red Indian babies called?
CLEVER DICK: Squawkers.

GEOGRAPHY TEACHER: What is a Laplander?
CLEVER DICK: Someone who falls over on a bus.

GEOGRAPHY TEACHER: What language do they speak in Cuba?
CLEVER DICK: Cubic?

GEOGRAPHY TEACHER: Can you give me three reasons why you know the world is round?
CLEVER DICK: Yes, sir. Mum says so, Dad says so, and you say so.

GEOGRAPHY TEACHER: What do you call the
small rivers that flow into the Nile?
CLEVER DICK: Juveniles?

GEOGRAPHY TEACHER: Find New Zealand on
the map for me, Johnny.
JOHNNY: There it is.
GEOGRAPHY TEACHER: Good. Now, Dick, can
you tell me who discovered New Zealand?
CLEVER DICK: Yes, sir. Johnny did.

GEOGRAPHY TEACHER: Why do Eskimos live
on whale meat and blubber?
CLEVER DICK: You'd cry too if you had to eat
whale meat all the time.

GEOGRAPHY TEACHER: What is the wettest
place in Britain?
CLEVER DICK: Bath.

GEOGRAPHY TEACHER: Did you know
Christopher Columbus discovered America?
CLEVER DICK: I didn't even know it was lost!

GEOGRAPHY TEACHER: Now, I will use my hat
to represent the planet Venus. Are there any
questions?
CLEVER DICK: Yes, sir. Is Venus inhabited?

GEOGRAPHY TEACHER: Where are the Andes?
CLEVER DICK: At the ends of the armies!

GEOGRAPHY TEACHER: A comet is a star with a
tail. Can anybody name one?
CLEVER DICK: Lassie!

GEOGRAPHY TEACHER: Why does the Statue of Liberty stand in New York harbour?
CLEVER DICK: Because it can't sit down.

GEOGRAPHY TEACHER: Where's Turkey?

CLEVER DICK: I'm sorry, sir, but we ate it all last Christmas.

GEOGRAPHY TEACHER: Where does it never rain?

CLEVER DICK: Under an umbrella!

GEOGRAPHY TEACHER: Where is Timbucktu?

CLEVER DICK: Somewhere between Timbuck-one and Timbuck-three.

GEOGRAPHY TEACHER: What shape is the world?

CLEVER DICK: Round.

GEOGRAPHY TEACHER: How do we know it is round?

CLEVER DICK: All right, it's square then. I don't want to start an argument!

GEOGRAPHY TEACHER: What is your favourite country?

CLEVER DICK: Czechoslovakia.

GEOGRAPHY TEACHER: Spell it.

CLEVER DICK: On second thoughts, I think I prefer Spain.

GEOGRAPHY TEACHER: What was the highest mountain in the world before Mount Everest was discovered?

CLEVER DICK: Mount Everest, of course.

GEOGRAPHY TEACHER: How would you describe the rain in the Amazon jungle?

CLEVER DICK: Little drops of water falling from the sky.

GEOGRAPHY TEACHER: Where is Felixstowe?
CLEVER DICK: At the end of Felix's foot.

CLEVER DICK: Do you know the capital of Alaska?
GEOGRAPHY TEACHER: Juneau?
CLEVER DICK: Yes, of course, but I'm asking you.

HISTORY TEACHER: What was the most remarkable achievement of the Romans?
CLEVER DICK: Learning Latin.

HISTORY TEACHER: What did Robert the Bruce do after he watched the spider climbing up and down?
CLEVER DICK: Er, invent the yo-yo?

HISTORY TEACHER: What did Caesar say when Brutus stabbed him?
CLEVER DICK: Ouch!

HISTORY TEACHER: Can you tell me what happened in 1939?
CLEVER DICK: Sorry, I can't remember that far back.

HISTORY TEACHER: Where did Captain Cook stand when he discovered Australia?
CLEVER DICK: On his feet.

HISTORY TEACHER: On what date did Columbus cross the Atlantic Ocean?
CLEVER DICK: He didn't cross on a date. He crossed on a ship.

HISTORY TEACHER: What did Julius Caesar do before crossing the Rubicon?
CLEVER DICK: Get in the boat.

HISTORY TEACHER: Why was Charles Dickens buried at Westminster Abbey?
CLEVER DICK: Because he was dead.

HISTORY TEACHER: In what year did William Shakespeare die?
CLEVER DICK: Die? I didn't even know he was sick.

HISTORY TEACHER: Where were the kings and queens of England crowned?
CLEVER DICK: On their heads.

HISTORY TEACHER: Where was the Magna Carta signed?
CLEVER DICK: At the bottom.

HISTORY TEACHER: Who can tell me something of importance that did not exist a hundred years ago?
CLEVER DICK: Me.

HISTORY TEACHER: Why were the Middle Ages called the Dark Ages?
CLEVER DICK: Because there were lots of knights then.

HISTORY TEACHER: How long was Elizabeth the First on the throne?
CLEVER DICK: The same length as she was when she was off it.

HISTORY TEACHER: In what battle was King Harold killed in 1066?

CLEVER DICK: His last one.

HISTORY TEACHER: At your age I could name all the English monarchs in the correct order.

CLEVER DICK: Yes, but in those days there had only been three or four of them.

HISTORY TEACHER: Why did King Arthur have a round table?

CLEVER DICK: So he couldn't get cornered.

HISTORY TEACHER: When was Rome built?

CLEVER DICK: At night.

HISTORY TEACHER: Why do you say that?

CLEVER DICK: Because I read somewhere that Rome wasn't built in a day.

HISTORY TEACHER: Who can name the Tudor kings and queens?

GIRL: Henry VII, Henry VIII, Edward VI, Mary ... er, that's all I know.

HISTORY TEACHER: Correct so far. Who can say who came after Mary?

CLEVER DICK: Her little lamb.

HISTORY TEACHER: For what was William Pitt the Elder chiefly responsible?

CLEVER DICK: William Pitt the Younger.

HISTORY TEACHER: Why did the Romans build straight roads?

CLEVER DICK: So the Britons couldn't hide round corners.

HISTORY TEACHER: Were there any great men born in our town?

CLEVER DICK: No, sir — only little babies.

HISTORY TEACHER: Who was MacAdam?

CLEVER DICK: The first Scotsman.

HISTORY TEACHER: What did Dick Turpin say at the end of his famous ride to York?

CLEVER DICK: Whoa!

HISTORY TEACHER: When was the Iron Age?

CLEVER DICK: Before the invention of drip dry shirts.

HISTORY TEACHER: Why did prehistoric men draw pictures of animals on the walls of their caves?

CLEVER DICK: Because they didn't know how to spell their names.

HISTORY TEACHER: George Washington not only chopped down his father's cherry tree, but he also admitted doing it. Now do you know why his father didn't punish him?

CLEVER DICK: Because George still had the axe in his hand.

HISTORY TEACHER: Who shot Abraham Lincoln?

CLEVER DICK: Sorry, sir, I don't split on anyone.

MATHS TEACHER: Can you tell me what comes before seven?

CLEVER DICK: Yes, sir, the milkman.

MATHS TEACHER: How many sides has a circle?

CLEVER DICK: Two — and outside and an inside.

MATHS TEACHER: If it takes three men twelve hours to build a brick wall, how long would it take six men to build it?

CLEVER DICK: No time at all. The three men just did it!

MATHS TEACHER: If you lost four fingers in an accident, what would you have?

CLEVER DICK: No more piano lessons.

MATHS TEACHER: Dick, are you copying Jim's sums?

CLEVER DICK: No, sir, I was just looking to see if he'd got mine right.

MATHS TEACHER: How many feet in a yard?

CLEVER DICK: Depends how many people are standing in it.

MATHS TEACHER: How old would someone be if they were born in 1952?

CLEVER DICK: Er . . . man or woman?

MATHS TEACHER: If you had six apples and someone took three of them, what would you have?

CLEVER DICK: A fight.

MATHS TEACHER: If I had fifty apples in one hand and fifty in the other, what would I have?

CLEVER DICK: Jolly big hands.

MATHS TEACHER: If you had to multiply twenty-seven by thirty-nine, what would you get?

CLEVER DICK: The wrong answer.

MATHS TEACHER: If you had six bars of chocolate and your friend asked for one of them, how many would you have left?

CLEVER DICK: Six.

SCIENCE TEACHER: The sun will last another hundred million years.

CLEVER DICK: So it should – we hardly use it.

SCIENCE TEACHER: If a person's brain stops working, does he die?
CLEVER DICK: Well, Billy's still alive, isn't he?

SCIENCE TEACHER: Why is the sea salty?
CLEVER DICK: Because the fish sweat so much.

SCIENCE TEACHER: What would you get if you swallowed uranium?
CLEVER DICK: Atomic ache.

SCIENCE TEACHER: What is the most important thing to remember in chemistry?
CLEVER DICK: Don't lick the spoon!

SCIENCE TEACHER: What did James Watt discover when he saw steam coming from the kettle?
CLEVER DICK: That it was time to make the tea.

CLEVER DICK: Sir, if I plant this pip in the garden will it grow into an orange tree?
SCIENCE TEACHER: It might do, yes.
CLEVER DICK: That's funny, it's an apple pip.

SCIENCE TEACHER: If we breathe oxygen during the daytime, what do we breathe at night?
CLEVER DICK: Nitrogen?

SCIENCE TEACHER: We all sprang from monkeys.
CLEVER DICK: But some of us didn't spring far enough.

SCIENCE TEACHER: What is the centre of gravity?

CLEVER DICK: The letter V!

CLEVER DICK: I have nearly 2000 bones in my body.

SCIENCE TEACHER: You know that's not possible.

CLEVER DICK: Yes it is. I had a tin of sardines for lunch!

SCIENCE TEACHER: What can you tell me about nitrates?

CLEVER DICK: They're cheaper than day rates, Miss.

SCIENCE TEACHER: What is the speed of light?

CLEVER DICK: I don't know, sir, but it must be very fast. It certainly reaches earth too early in the morning.

SCIENCE TEACHER: What is water, Dick?

CLEVER DICK: It's a colourless liquid that turns black when I put my hands in it.

SCIENCE TEACHER: Who can name a deadly poison?

CLEVER DICK: Aviation. One drop and you're dead.

SCIENCE TEACHER: Light from the sun travels at a speed of 186,000 miles a second. Isn't that remarkable?

CLEVER DICK: I don't know — it's downhill all the way.

SCIENCE TEACHER: What are bacteria?
CLEVER DICK: The rear entrances to cafeterias.

NATURAL HISTORY TEACHER: What do you call the outer part of a tree?
CLEVER DICK: I don't know, sir.
NATURAL HISTORY TEACHER: Bark, boy, bark.
CLEVER DICK: Woof, woof.

NATURAL HISTORY TEACHER: Why do lions eat raw meat?
CLEVER DICK: Because they don't know how to cook.

NATURAL HISTORY TEACHER: Did you know it takes three sheep to make a sweater?
CLEVER DICK: No, miss – I didn't even know sheep could knit.

NATURAL HISTORY TEACHER: What bird has wings but cannot fly?
CLEVER DICK: Roast turkey.

NATURAL HISTORY TEACHER: What's the difference between an Indian elephant and an African elephant?
CLEVER DICK: About 3000 miles.

NATURAL HISTORY TEACHER: Can you tell me some of the uses of cowhide?
CLEVER DICK: Yes, it keeps the cow together.

NATURAL HISTORY TEACHER: Name four members of the cat family.
CLEVER DICK: Father cat, Mother cat, and their two kittens.

NATURAL HISTORY TEACHER: What are the biggest ants in the world?
CLEVER DICK: Gi-ants and eleph-ants.

NATURAL HISTORY TEACHER: What do we get from whales?
CLEVER DICK: Coal, sir.
NATURAL HISTORY TEACHER: No, not Wales. I mean whales in the sea.
CLEVER DICK: Oh, sea coal, sir.

NATURAL HISTORY TEACHER: To what family does the rhinoceros belong?
CLEVER DICK: I don't know, but I'm sure it's no family in my street!

Clever Dick and School Reports

MOTHER: I'm very worried about you being at the bottom of the class.
CLEVER DICK: You needn't worry, Mum. They teach the same stuff as at the top.

MOTHER: Sit down and tell me what your school report is like.
CLEVER DICK: I can't sit down. I've just told Dad.

FATHER: Well, did you get a good place in your exams?
CLEVER DICK: Yes, Dad — right next to the radiator.

FATHER: Did you pass your exams?
CLEVER DICK: No, but I was top of those that failed.

MOTHER: What did your father say when he
saw your school report?
CLEVER DICK: Shall I leave out the bad
language?
MOTHER: Of course.
CLEVER DICK: He didn't say a word.

FATHER: You've failed your exams again! How do you think you're ever going to get up to A level?

CLEVER DICK: Perhaps I could use a lift.

FATHER: Your report is very bad this term, Dick. What happened?

CLEVER DICK: Oh, that's the teacher's fault.

FATHER: Why is that?

CLEVER DICK: Well, I used to sit next to Michael who is top of the class, but the teacher moved me.

TEACHER: In the exam you will be allowed half an hour for each question.

CLEVER DICK: And how long are we allowed for each answer?

FATHER: Why do you always fail your exams?

CLEVER DICK: Because they always give me the wrong papers.

CLEVER DICK SAYS: My mother suffers from a neurosis: every time she sees my school report she faints!

FATHER: Dick, I'm not at all pleased with this report!

CLEVER DICK: Yes, I told my teacher you wouldn't like it, but she insisted I brought it home just the same.

FATHER: How were your exam marks?

CLEVER DICK: Under water.

FATHER: What do you mean, 'under water'?

CLEVER DICK: Below C level!

114

FRIEND: What's your brother going to be when he passes his exam?

CLEVER DICK: An old age pensioner.

MOTHER: What does this F mean on your report, Dick?

CLEVER DICK: Fantastic?

FATHER: What's all this? Your school report says that your teacher finds it impossible to teach you anything.

CLEVER DICK: I told you he was no good.

FATHER: This report is terrible. It says here that you are nothing but a little pest. What does that mean?

CLEVER DICK: Perhaps it means I'm the son of a big pest.

CLEVER DICK: Dad is suffering from a low grade infection.

FRIEND: What does that mean?

CLEVER DICK: Every time he sees my report he gets sick!

CLEVER DICK: Remember you promised me ten pounds if I passed my exams?

FATHER: Yes . . .

CLEVER DICK: Well I've got great news. You've just saved ten pounds!

FATHER: I see you got an E for conduct but an A for courtesy. How on earth did you manage that?

CLEVER DICK: Whenever I kick someone I apologize.

Clever Dick and Homework

TEACHER: Your homework seems to be in your father's handwriting.

CLEVER DICK: Yes, sir, that's probably because I used his pen.

TEACHER: Tell me the truth: who did your homework?

CLEVER DICK: My father.

TEACHER: Really! It's all wrong!

CLEVER DICK: Well, I helped him with it.

TEACHER: Where's your homework?

CLEVER DICK: In the dustbin.

TEACHER: Why?

CLEVER DICK: My father said it was a load of rubbish.

TEACHER: Your homework is definitely getting better.

CLEVER DICK: Yes, that's because my Dad has stopped helping me.

FATHER: Why are you writing your homework so slowly?

CLEVER DICK: Because my teacher can't read very fast.

TEACHER: Why do you look so tired?

CLEVER DICK: I was up till twelve doing my homework.

TEACHER: What time did you start?

CLEVER DICK: Eleven fifty-five.

TEACHER: Where's your homework, Dick?
CLEVER DICK: I made it into a paper plane and someone hijacked it.

TEACHER: Did your father help you with your homework?
CLEVER DICK: No, miss, I got it wrong all by myself.

COOKERY TEACHER: What's the best way to serve leftovers?
CLEVER DICK: To somebody else.

COOKERY TEACHER: How do you make a sausage roll?
CLEVER DICK: Push it.

COOKERY TEACHER: How do you make a Swiss roll?
CLEVER DICK: Push him down an Alp.

COOKERY TEACHER: How can we prevent food from going bad?
CLEVER DICK: By eating it.

CLEVER DICK: My Dad's motorbike can cook eggs.
COOKERY TEACHER: Really, what type of motorbike is it?
CLEVER DICK: A scrambler.

CLEVER DICK: Miss, have you heard the joke about the three eggs?
COOKERY TEACHER: No.
CLEVER DICK: Two bad.

COOKERY TEACHER: How long do you cook spaghetti?

CLEVER DICK: Oh, about ten inches.

COOKERY TEACHER: I made a beef casserole and the school cat has just eaten it.

CLEVER DICK: Never mind, miss, we can easily get another cat.

COOKERY TEACHER: At a buffet party, should one serve boiled eggs?

CLEVER DICK: One should serve whoever shows up.

COOKERY TEACHER: How do you keep rice from sticking together?

CLEVER DICK: Boil each grain separately.

COOKERY TEACHER: What's a good way of keeping your food bills down?

CLEVER DICK: Using a heavier paperweight.

CLEVER DICK: If we sold our art teacher we could get a lot of money.

ART PUPIL: How could we do that?

CLEVER DICK: It says in today's newspaper that Old Masters are fetching record prices at auctions.

WOODWORK TEACHER: What are you making, Dick?

CLEVER DICK: A portable, sir.

WOODWORK TEACHER: A portable what?

CLEVER DICK: I don't know yet — so far I've only made the handle.

3 Clever Dick At Large

Clever Dick at the Disco

BOY: Until I met you, life was just one big
  desert.
CLEVER DICK GIRL: Is that why you dance like
  a camel?

GIRL: Darling, I want to dance like this
  forever.
CLEVER DICK: Don't you ever want to improve?

GIRL: Dancers run in my family.
CLEVER DICK: Too bad they don't dance.

BOY: I never danced so badly before.
CLEVER DICK GIRL: Oh, then you have danced
  before?

BOY: May I have the last dance?
CLEVER DICK GIRL: You've just had it.

BOY: Today I danced like I never danced
  before.
CLEVER DICK GIRL: Oh, I see, on your own
  feet.

CLEVER DICK: You would be a great dancer except for two things.
PARTNER: What are they?
CLEVER DICK: Your feet!

Clever Dick Eating Out

MAN IN RESTAURANT: Do you mind if I smoke?
CLEVER DICK: Not if you don't mind me being sick.

CUSTOMER: Waiter, why have you got your finger on my steak?
CLEVER DICK WAITER: To stop it falling on the floor again.

WAITER: We have almost everything on the menu, sir.
CLEVER DICK: So I see. Could I have a clean one, please?

CLEVER DICK: How much is lunch at this restaurant?
WAITER: £20 a head, sir.
CLEVER DICK: Just bring me an ear, then.

CLEVER DICK: Are waiters supposed to be tipped?
WAITER: Of course.
CLEVER DICK: Good, then tip me. I've been waiting for service for half an hour!

WAITER: How did you find your steak, sir?
CLEVER DICK: I looked under a chip, and there it was!

CLEVER DICK: This restaurant must have a very clean kitchen.
WAITER: Thank you. What makes you say that?
CLEVER DICK: Everything tastes of soap.

WAITER: Would you like a lemon with your tea?
CLEVER DICK: No thanks, I prefer to be alone.

WAITER: How do you like your steak, sir?
CLEVER DICK: Big.

WAITER: How did you find your steak, madam?
CLEVER DICK GIRL: With a magnifying glass.

CUSTOMER: What do I have to do to get a glass of water in this place?
CLEVER DICK WAITER: Set yourself on fire.

MAN IN RESTAURANT: Do you mind if I smoke?
CLEVER DICK: Sir, I don't care if you burn!

FRIEND: This is good soup.
CLEVER DICK: Yes, it sounds good!

FRIEND: Will you join me in a bowl of soup?
CLEVER DICK: Do you think there's room for both of us?

CLEVER DICK TO WAITER: Is this steak well done, or has it been cremated?

CLEVER DICK: Can you bring me some hot water please?
WAITER: Do you want to rinse your fingers?
CLEVER DICK: No, I want to wash the cutlery.

CLEVER DICK TO WAITER: When you described this as original Indian food, I didn't realize that meant it was cooked there in the first place.

WAITER: I have stewed liver, boiled tongue, and frog's legs.

CLEVER DICK: Don't tell me your problems, just bring me the menu.

CLEVER DICK TO WAITER: I asked for some soup twenty minutes ago — are you having trouble opening the tin?

CLEVER DICK TO WAITER: Is this rice or were they maggots?

CLEVER DICK TO WAITER: Can you take this away, please. I think it's the same meal I rejected last time I was here.

CLEVER DICK TO WAITER: Has the electricity been cut off? I asked for a hot meal.

CLEVER DICK TO WAITER: Do you serve indigestion tablets with every course?

BONUS INSULTS: HOW TO BE RUDE TO A WAITER *AND* EMBARRASS YOUR PARENTS

Sometimes it's possible to kill two birds with one stone. If you're lucky enough to be taken out to a restaurant, you're being handed the perfect opportunity on a plate (ha ha). Try these for starters (ho ho):

CLEVER DICK: Do you run your own hospital for people who eat here?

CLEVER DICK: Has the chef been having a bath in this soup?

CLEVER DICK: Do you supply a magnifying glass with your chips?

CLEVER DICK: Do you kill your own cabbage here?

CLEVER DICK: I asked for pancakes, not cowcakes.

CLEVER DICK: How many people chewed this steak before I got it?

CLEVER DICK: Do you keep pigs in here between mealtimes?

CLEVER DICK: You deserve a tip. The tip of my boot!

An expert Clever Dick will not only be cheeky to people to their faces, but will pepper everyday conversation with millions of barbed quips and catty comments.

Memorize one or two every day, and you'll soon be able to boldly insult where no man has insulted before!

CLEVER DICK: You should be a boxer.
VICTIM: Why?
CLEVER DICK: Someone might knock you unconscious.

CLEVER DICK: You're the type that attracts raving beauties.
VICTIM: Really?
CLEVER DICK: Yes, escapees from the loony bin!

CLEVER DICK: Is your stomach all right?
VICTIM: Yes, why?
CLEVER DICK: I just wondered if it was as sour as your face.

CLEVER DICK: You should be on the stage.
VICTIM: You really think so?
CLEVER DICK: Yes, there's one leaving in five minutes.

CLEVER DICK: There's no point telling you a joke with a double meaning.
VICTIM: Why not?
CLEVER DICK: You wouldn't get either of them.

CLEVER DICK: We're going to Majorca this year.

VICTIM: Flying?

CLEVER DICK: No, we're going by plane.

CLEVER DICK: You'd make a great parole officer.

VICTIM: Why do you say that?

CLEVER DICK: You never let anyone finish a sentence.

CLEVER DICK: I'll give this pound to anybody who is quite contented.

VICTIM: I'm quite contented.

CLEVER DICK: Then why do you want my pound?

CLEVER DICK: Do you know that the most intelligent person in the world has gone deaf?

VICTIM: No. Why is that?

CLEVER DICK: Pardon?

CLEVER DICK: How do you keep the school idiot in suspense?

VICTIM: I don't know. How?

CLEVER DICK: I'll tell you tomorrow.

CLEVER DICK: You'd make a perfect . . .

VICTIM: Perfect what?

CLEVER DICK: Stranger!

CLEVER DICK: Did you hear the joke about the rope?

VICTIM: No.

CLEVER DICK: Skip it!

CLEVER DICK: I'd never go swimming in a concrete swimming pool
VICTIM: Why not?
CLEVER DICK: I don't like swimming in concrete.

CLEVER DICK: I've invented a new kind of coffin that just covers the head.
VICTIM: What's the good of that?
CLEVER DICK: It's for people like you — dead from the neck up!

CLEVER DICK: You remind me of a man.

VICTIM: What man?

CLEVER DICK: The man with the power.

VICTIM: What power?

CLEVER DICK: The power of 'oo-do'.

VICTIM: Who do?

CLEVER DICK: You do!

VICTIM: I do what?

CLEVER DICK: Remind me of a man.

VICTIM: What man?

CLEVER DICK: The man with the power . . .

Clever Dick and Friends

CLEVER DICK: Where do you bathe?

OUTDOOR FRIEND: In the spring.

CLEVER DICK: I said where, not when!

CLEVER DICK: Do you have a good seat?

FRIEND: Yes, thank you.

CLEVER DICK: You can see all right?

FRIEND: Yes, fine thanks.

CLEVER DICK: There's nobody blocking your view?

FRIEND: No.

CLEVER DICK: Sure?

FRIEND: Positive.

CLEVER DICK: Will you change places with me, then?

CLEVER DICK: Would you like some nougat?

FRIEND: It's pronounced noogar. The T is silent.

CLEVER DICK: Not the way you drink it, it isn't!

FRIEND: My new girlfriend's a slick chick!
CLEVER DICK: You mean she's like a greasy chicken?

CLEVER DICK: We've just got a new dog. Would you like to come and see him?
FRIEND: Does he bite?
CLEVER DICK: That's what I'm trying to find out.

FRIEND: I can lie in bed and watch the sun rise.
CLEVER DICK: That's nothing. I can sit on a stool and watch the kitchen sink!

FRIEND: Did your watch stop when you dropped it on the floor?
CLEVER DICK: Of course! Did you think it would go right through the ground?

FRIEND: I have a terrible problem. Can you help me out?
CLEVER DICK: Certainly. Which way did you come in?

CLEVER DICK TO FRIEND: Aren't you ever tired of having yourself around?

FRIEND: Weren't you ever homesick?
CLEVER DICK: Not me – I never stay there that long.

FRIEND: How much money do you have in the bank?
CLEVER DICK: I don't know, I haven't shaken it lately.

FRIEND: Did you hear my last joke?
CLEVER DICK: I certainly hope so!

FRIEND: I choose my own clothes.
CLEVER DICK: That's funny, I've got moths that chew mine.

FRIEND: Do you play the piano by ear?
CLEVER DICK: No, I play it by the window, to annoy the neighbours.

FRIEND: I'll tell you a joke that will kill you.
CLEVER DICK: Please don't! I'm too young to die!

FRIEND: What's the name of your new baby sister?
CLEVER DICK: I don't know. I can't understand a word she says.

FRIEND: What would you do if you were in my shoes?
CLEVER DICK: Polish them.

FRIEND: Where did you learn how to swim?
CLEVER DICK: In the water.

FRIEND: Can you keep a straight face while telling a lie?
CLEVER DICK: No, my lips always move.

FRIEND: How far is your house from the station?
CLEVER DICK: About a ten minute walk, if you run.

CLEVER DICK TO FRIEND: I've got a couple of minutes to kill. Why not tell me everything you know?

FRIEND: Shall we play horse?
CLEVER DICK: Okay, I'll be the head and you just be yourself.

FRIEND: I don't think the photo you took of me does me justice.
CLEVER DICK: You don't want justice, you want mercy!

FRIEND: I've got a head cold. How can I stop it from going to my chest?
CLEVER DICK: Tie a knot in your neck.

FRIEND: My mother almost lost me as a child.
CLEVER DICK: Didn't she take you far enough into the woods?

FRIEND: What do you mean, Yuletide Greetings?
CLEVER DICK: Lend me a fiver, and you'll tide me over till Christmas!

CLEVER DICK TO FRIEND: I'd like to say you're a wonderful singer. I'd like to . . . but I never lie.

FRIEND: Why did you paint my portrait in oil?
CLEVER DICK: Because you have a face like a sardine.

FRIEND: I was born on April 2nd.
CLEVER DICK: A day too late.

FRIEND: How long can you live without a brain?
CLEVER DICK: I don't know. How old are you?

FRIEND: Have you heard the saying, 'A friend in need is a friend indeed'?
CLEVER DICK: Yes, stranger.

FRIEND: Can you stand on your head?
CLEVER DICK: No, it's too high.

FRIEND: Why are you standing on your head?
CLEVER DICK: I'm turning things over in my mind.

FRIEND: How do you catch dandruff?
CLEVER DICK: Shake your head over a paper bag.

CLEVER DICK: I don't think my mother likes me.
FRIEND: Why's that?
CLEVER DICK: She keeps wrapping up my sandwiches in a road map.

CLEVER DICK: I don't think either of my parents like me.
FRIEND: Why?
CLEVER DICK: When I got home from school yesterday I found they'd moved house.

CLEVER DICK: I think you should become a doctor.
FRIEND: Really?
CLEVER DICK: Yes, you've got the handwriting for it.

CLEVER DICK: A tramp came up to me in the street and said he hadn't had a bite for days.

FRIEND: What did you do?

CLEVER DICK: I let Rover off the lead.

CLEVER DICK: Do you feel like a cup of tea?

FRIEND: Oh, yes.

CLEVER DICK: I thought so. You look sloppy, wet and hot!

FRIEND: Our dog is just like one of the family.

CLEVER DICK: Really? Which one?

FRIEND: Is it bad to write on an empty stomach?

CLEVER DICK: No, but it's better to write on paper.

FRIEND: What was the funniest thing you ever saw?

CLEVER DICK: The first time you walked into a room.

FRIEND: Who's that little lady with the wart?

CLEVER DICK: She's his wife.

FRIEND: Jim's not very clever. I don't think he'll ever get a job.

CLEVER DICK: I don't know – he could always be a ventriloquist's dummy.

FRIEND: Is it really bad luck to have a black cat follow you?

CLEVER DICK: Depends whether you're a man or a mouse!

CLEVER DICK: Do you have holes in your trousers?

FRIEND: Of course not.

CLEVER DICK: Then how do you get your legs through?

FRIEND: How do you find my breath?
CLEVER DICK: Offensive – it's keeping you
alive.

CLEVER DICK TO FRIEND: Have you been to the
zoo? I mean, as a visitor.

CLEVER DICK: If frozen water is iced water,
what is frozen ink?
FRIEND: Iced ink.
CLEVER DICK: I know you do!

FRIEND: A funny thing happened to my mother
in London.
CLEVER DICK: But I thought you were born in
Manchester?

FRIEND: I keep talking to myself.
CLEVER DICK: No wonder. No one else would
listen to you.

FRIEND: I always like to think the best of
people.
CLEVER DICK: That's why I think of you as an
imbecile!

FRIEND: I often wonder what my IQ is.
CLEVER DICK: Don't worry about it, it's
nothing.

CLEVER DICK: I feel sorry for your poor little
mind.
FRIEND: Why?
CLEVER DICK: All alone in that great big
head . . .

FRIEND: Let's play a game of wits.
CLEVER DICK: No, let's choose one you can play too!

FRIEND: I definitely have a mind of my own.
CLEVER DICK: Of course you do. No one else would want it!

FRIEND: The doctor examined my head yesterday.
CLEVER DICK: Did he find anything in it?

FRIEND: I never act stupid.
CLEVER DICK: No — with you, it's the real thing.

FRIEND: I'm thinking hard.
CLEVER DICK: Don't you mean it's hard for you to think?

FRIEND: I think faster than you.
CLEVER DICK: I can tell. You've stopped already.

FRIEND: I have a ready wit.
CLEVER DICK: Let me know when you're ready.

FRIEND: My mum's gone on a crash diet.
CLEVER DICK: I can tell — she certainly looks like a wreck!

FRIEND: Before I was born, my father wanted a boy and my mother wanted a girl.
CLEVER DICK: So with you, they can both be satisfied!

FRIEND: George comes up with an answer for every problem.

CLEVER DICK: But it's always wrong!

FRIEND: Will you join me?

CLEVER DICK: Why, are you coming apart?

FRIEND: My sister's not too bad when you get to know her.

CLEVER DICK: But who wants to know her?

FRIEND: Is it raining outside?
CLEVER DICK: Did it ever rain inside?

FRIEND: How did you sleep last night?
CLEVER DICK: As usual, with my eyes closed.

FRIEND: Do you ever snore?
CLEVER DICK: Only when I'm asleep.

FRIEND: You shouldn't be swimming on a full stomach.
CLEVER DICK: I'll swim on my back.

BORING FRIEND: Hello, what's going on?
CLEVER DICK (*moving off*): I am.

FRIEND: I want to give you my opinion, for what it's worth.
CLEVER DICK: In that case you owe me 2p.

FRIEND: Words fail me.
CLEVER DICK: That's because of the way you use them.

Clever Dick and Boasters

BOASTER: I've hunted bear – have you?
CLEVER DICK: No, but I've gone fishing in my shorts.

BOASTER: I'm a well-known collector of antiques.
CLEVER DICK: I know. I've seen your wife.

BOASTER: My girlfriend has lots of personality.
CLEVER DICK: Mine isn't too good looking either.

BOASTER: I used to be with the circus.
CLEVER DICK: What cage were you in?

BOASTER: I've got a barometer that was made in America.
CLEVER DICK: So who needs to know when it's raining in New York?

BOASTER: I got up at dawn yesterday to see the sunrise.
CLEVER DICK: Well, you couldn't have picked a better time.

BOASTER: My sister has got engaged to an X-ray scientist.
CLEVER DICK: I wonder what he sees in her?

BOASTER: My rich uncle owns a newspaper.
CLEVER DICK: So what? A newspaper only costs 20p.

BOASTER: I play by ear.
CLEVER DICK: I listen the same way.

BOASTER: I'm going to buy something nice in oil for my house.
CLEVER DICK: A painting or a tin of sardines?

BOASTER: I fired my gun and there was a dead lion at my feet.
CLEVER DICK: How long had he been dead?

BOASTER: I went to Hollywood and made two pictures at the same time.

CLEVER DICK: Your first and your last?

BOASTER: It could take ten men to fill my shoes.

CLEVER DICK: It certainly looks as though it took ten cows to make them!

BOASTER: I've been tracing my ancestors. I'm descended from royalty.

CLEVER DICK: King Kong?

BOASTER: Girls fall in love with me at first sight.

CLEVER DICK: Yes, it's when they take a second look that they can't stand you!

BOASTER: Girls whisper that they love me.

CLEVER DICK: You don't think they'd admit it out loud, do you?

BOASTER: Every time I pass a girl she sighs.

CLEVER DICK: With relief!

BOASTING GIRL: I was selected by a computer as an ideal girlfriend.

CLEVER DICK: Who wants to be a computer's girlfriend?

BOASTER: I have a clear mind.

CLEVER DICK: You mean, it's not cluttered up with information?

BOASTER: I'm good at everything I do.

CLEVER DICK: Yes, and as far as I can see you usually do nothing!

BOASTER: On my new radio I can get Brazil and Peru.

CLEVER DICK: That's nothing. I can stick my head out of the window and get chilly!

BOASTER: I do lots of exercise.

CLEVER DICK: I can tell — you're certainly long-winded!

BOASTER: My sister is beautiful.

CLEVER DICK: Yes, like a Greek statue — beautiful, but not all there.

BOASTER: My brother's been at university for years.

CLEVER DICK: I know, he's got more degrees than a thermometer.

BOASTER: I speak eight languages.

CLEVER DICK: Unfortunately, all at the same time.

BOASTER: I'm not afraid of the dark.

CLEVER DICK: As long as the light's left on.

BOASTER: When I was born they fired a twenty-one gun salute.

CLEVER DICK: Pity they missed.

BOASTER: One of my relatives died at Waterloo.

CLEVER DICK: Really? Which platform?

BOASTING MUM: My baby is a year old today, and she's been walking since she was nine months old.

CLEVER DICK: Really? She must be very tired!

BOASTER: My brother's a real big gun in industry.

CLEVER DICK: He should be careful or they might fire him.

BOASTER: I have very keen senses.

CLEVER DICK: All except one – common sense!

BOASTER: I'm going to give my dad a cordless shaver for Christmas.

CLEVER DICK: Yeah, a sheet of coarse sandpaper!

BOASTER: I'm going to have a dog for Christmas.

CLEVER DICK: Really? We're going to have a turkey as usual!

BOASTER: My dad's so rich, I don't know what to buy him for Christmas. What do you give to a man who has everything?

CLEVER DICK: A burglar alarm?

BOASTER: My girlfriend gave me a present that made my eyes pop out.

CLEVER DICK: Yeah, a shirt with a collar three sizes too small!

BOASTER: I can trace my family tree way back.

CLEVER DICK: Yeah, back to the time you lived in it!

BOASTER: I gave my mother a twelve-piece set of silver for Christmas.

CLEVER DICK: Eleven 5ps and a 10p.

BOASTER: I've just received a film offer from
   Hollywood.
CLEVER DICK: I'm not surprised. There can't be
   that many people who can play Frankenstein's
   monster without make-up.

BOASTER: I made a couple of pictures in
    Hollywood.
CLEVER DICK: When do you get them back from
    the chemist?

BOASTING WOMAN: I wanted to marry a big
    movie star or nothing.
CLEVER DICK: You got your wish, then —
    married a big nothing.

BOASTER: My brother is the kind of guy that
    girls dream of.
CLEVER DICK: That's better than seeing him by
    daylight.

BOASTER: I was born with a silver spoon in my
    mouth.
CLEVER DICK: That's funny, normal kids have
    tongues!

BOASTER: I'm the teacher's pet.
CLEVER DICK: Can't she afford a cat?

SNAPPY COMEBACKS

Often, the person you're talking to will 'feed' you
    with a great chance for a quick insult. Here
    are some golden examples.

FRIEND: I like to throw myself into everything
    I do.
CLEVER DICK: Good, then go and dig a big hole.

MOTHER: Did you take a bath?
CLEVER DICK: Why? Is there one missing?

144

MOTHER: Have you heard, your uncle has lost his glasses?
CLEVER DICK: Yes, I suppose he'll have to drink straight from the bottle now.

FRIEND: I have a hunch.
CLEVER DICK: And here was me thinking you were just round-shouldered.

FRIEND: Sorry, my mind was wandering.
CLEVER DICK: Don't worry – it's too weak to go far.

FATHER: I never told lies when I was a child.
CLEVER DICK: So when did you begin?

FRIEND: Do you feel like a cup of tea?
CLEVER DICK: Of course not – do I look like one?

FRIEND: I don't know the meaning of fear.
CLEVER DICK: Why don't you look it up in the dictionary?

FRIEND: I'm so thirsty my tongue is hanging out.
CLEVER DICK: Gosh! I thought it was your tie!

MOTHER: Work hard and you'll get ahead.
CLEVER DICK: I've got a head.

FRIEND: My father is a blacksmith.
CLEVER DICK: So that's why you're forging ahead!

GIRL FRIEND: My father is a postman.

CLEVER DICK: No wonder you know your males!

FRIEND: Gill's father is in the church.

CLEVER DICK: No wonder you can't put anything pastor!

FRIEND: My father is an optician.

CLEVER DICK: Is that why you keep making a spectacle of yourself?

FRIEND: My father is a fireman.

CLEVER DICK: Go to blazes!

FRIEND: My father is a chimneysweep.

CLEVER DICK: Is that why you wear a soot?

FRIEND: Tracey's father is a tailor.

CLEVER DICK: No wonder she's always got pins and needles.

FRIEND: My father is an electrician.

CLEVER DICK: I expect you have good connections?

FRIEND: My father is a fisherman.

CLEVER DICK: So that's why all the girls seem to swallow your line.

FRIEND: Sharon's father is a draughtsman.

CLEVER DICK: Is that why she knows where to draw the line?

Clever Dick at the Doctor's

CLEVER DICK: A dog just bit me on my ankle.
DOCTOR: Did you put anything on it?
CLEVER DICK: No, he liked it just as it was!

CLEVER DICK: When my fingers heal, will I be able to play the piano?
DOCTOR: Of course.
CLEVER DICK: Fantastic! I never could before!

PATIENT: Doctor, doctor, I've broken my leg. What shall I do?
CLEVER DICK DOCTOR: Limp.

PATIENT: Doctor, doctor, can you give me something for my liver?
CLEVER DICK DOCTOR: How about some bacon and onions?

PATIENT: Doctor, doctor, my hair's falling out. Can you give me something to keep it in?
CLEVER DICK DOCTOR: Here's a paper bag.

DOCTOR: Have your eyes ever been checked?
CLEVER DICK: No, they've always been brown.

DOCTOR: I spent seven years at university taking medicine.
CLEVER DICK: Are you well now?

DOCTOR: Are you taking your medicine regularly?
CLEVER DICK: No, Doc. I tasted it and decided to keep on coughing.

DOCTOR: Tell me, were you ever troubled with diptheria?

CLEVER DICK: Only when I tried to spell it.

Clever Dick Out and About

CLEVER DICK (*visiting aunt in hospital*): I've brought you a box of your favourite chocolates.

AUNTY: Oh, wonderful! But the box is almost empty!

CLEVER DIC K: They're my favourites, too.

CLEVER DICK: Will this bus take me to Piccadilly?

CONDUCTOR: Which part?

CLEVER DICK: All of me, of course!

CLEVER DICK: Does this band take requests?

MUSICIAN: Certainly.

CLEVER DICK: Good. I request they stop playing.

JUDGE: Do you plead guilty or not guilty?

CLEVER DICK DEFENDANT: Any other choices?

JUDGE: The victim's wallet was inside his jacket. How did you manage to get it out?

CLEVER DICK DEFENDANT: Sorry, M'lud, but I charge £10 an hour for lessons.

JUDGE: This is the twentieth time I've had you up in front of me. I fine you £200.

CLEVER DICK DEFENDANT: Any chance of a discount for being a good customer?

JUDGE: Do you plead guilty or not guilty?
CLEVERDICK DEFENDANT: I'll let you know after I've heard the evidence.

JUDGE: What is your date of birth?
CLEVER DICK DEFENDANT: Why do you want to know? Sending me a birthday present?

HOTEL PORTER: Can I carry your bag, sir?
CLEVER DICK: No, let her walk!

CLEVER DICK: Do you make life-size enlargements?
PHOTOGRAPHER: Certainly we do, sir.
CLEVER DICK: Good. Here is a picture of an elephant.

POST OFFICE ASSISTANT: Shall I put the stamp on myself?
CLEVER DICK: No, on the letter.

CLEVER DICK IN ANTIQUE SHOP: Are these worm holes or did the Elizabethan owners use this as a dart-board?

CLEVER DICK IN BUTCHER'S: If that's a leg of lamb then its mother must have been crossed with a chihuahua.

CLEVER DICK AT THE GROCER'S: Either these raisins have seen better days or the mice in the shop have been eating well.

LANDOWNER: You're not allowed to fish here.
CLEVER DICK: I'm not fishing, I'm giving my pet worm a bath.

LANDOWNER: You're not allowed to fish here.
CLEVER DICK: I'm not fishing, I'm saving my pet worm from drowning.

FISHERMAN: You've been watching me for two hours. Why don't you try fishing yourself?
CLEVER DICK: I haven't got the patience.

FISHERMAN: Do you know the best way to catch a fish?
CLEVER DICK: Have someone throw it at you?

BIG STORE SANTA CLAUS: And what would you like for Christmas?
CLEVER DICK: I wrote to you last week, you fool. I knew you'd forget!

PASSENGER: Driver, does this bus stop at the river?
CLEVER DICK CONDUCTOR: If it doesn't there's going to be a mighty big splash!

CLEVER DICK ON THE PLANE: Excuse me, stewardess, is this Russian salad, or have you run out of the little bags?

CLEVER DICK (*getting out of taxi*): What do you mean, 'What about my tip'? I've just been travelling in it, that's what.

STRANGER: How do you get to the Albert Hall?
CLEVER DICK: Practice, sir, practice!

VISITOR: Do these stairs take you to the second floor?
CLEVER DICK: No, you'll have to walk.

VISITOR: Did you live here all your life?
CLEVER DICK: I don't know. I haven't died yet.

GROWN-UP: This is a dangerous world we live in.
CLEVER DICK: Yes, very few get out of it alive.

FRIEND: I guess we all just live and learn.
CLEVER DICK: Yes, but you just live.

VISITOR: What does your father do for a living?
CLEVER DICK: As little as possible.

FRIEND: I live by my wits.
CLEVER DICK: I thought you looked hungry!

FRIEND: Have you forgotten that you owe me £5?
CLEVER DICK: No, not yet. Give me time and I will.

MUM'S FRIEND: I'm going to give you a piece of my mind.
CLEVER DICK: Watch out now – you don't have much left.

FRIEND: Don't you hate people who talk behind your back?
CLEVER DICK: Yes, especially at the cinema.

ANGRY LADY: I thought you were supposed to come and fix the doorbell yesterday?
CLEVER DICK ELECTRICIAN: I did – I rang twice and got no answer.

BUS PASSENGER: Am I all right for the zoo?
CLEVER DICK CONDUCTOR: With your face, sir, you certainly are.

STRANGER: Can you play the piano?
CLEVER DICK: I don't know. I never tried.

BARBER: How do you want your hair cut?
CLEVER DICK: Off!

BARBER: You say you've been in my barbershop before. I don't remember your face.
CLEVER DICK: Oh, it's all healed up now.

GROCER: These are the best eggs we've had for years.
CLEVER DICK: Well, bring me some that you haven't had so long.

Clever Dick in Love

GIRL: Am I the first girl you ever kissed?
CLEVER DICK: Maybe – your face looks familiar.

BOY: May I see you pretty soon?
CLEVER DICK GIRL: Don't you think I'm pretty now?

CLEVER DICK TO GIRLFRIEND: Darling you look wonderful – what happened?

GIRL: What has she got that I haven't got?
CLEVER DICK: Shall I give it to you alphabetically?

GIRL: Where did you get those big eyes?
CLEVER DICK: They came with the face.

153

BOY: Darling, the whole world revolves around you.

CLEVER DICK GIRL: Well, I told you not to drink that beer!

CLEVER DICK TO GIRLFRIEND: I'd like to run my fingers through your hair. Can you remember where you left it?

SISTER: Jack is the sweetest, most darling husband in all the world.

CLEVER DICK: Too bad you married George.

BOY: Should a boy kiss with his eyes closed?

CLEVER DICK GIRL: No, kiss her with your lips.

BOY: I love you terribly.

CLEVER DICK GIRL: You certainly do!

GIRL: Kate is in love.

CLEVER DICK: That's nothing. Sydney is in Australia.

CLEVER DICK SAYS: My girlfriend has such beautiful hair, every time we go out I insist that she wears it.

TRACEY: Whisper those three little words that will make me walk on air.

CLEVER DICK: Go hang yourself!

FRIEND: Why do you call your boyfriend laryngitis?

CLEVER DICK GIRL: Because he's a pain in the neck.

GIRL: If you were my husband I'd give you poison.

CLEVER DICK: If you were my wife I'd take it.

GIRL: I'd like you better if you were tall, dark and handsome.
CLEVER DICK: If I was tall, dark and handsome I wouldn't be going around with you.

FRED: Jane and I met in a revolving door.
CLEVER DICK: And I suppose you've been going round together ever since?

PASSIONATE FRENCH GIRL: *Je t'adore* . . .
CLEVER DICK: Shut it yourself!

DEBBIE: If you don't say you love me, I'll blow my brains out.
CLEVER DICK: Go on then, you've got nothing to lose.

GLENDA: Am I really as pretty as a picture?
CLEVER DICK: Yes, but your frame's in a bit of a mess.

CLEVER DICK: My girlfriend has got pedestrian eyes.
FRIEND: Pedestrian eyes?
CLEVER DICK: Yes, they look both ways before they cross.

GEORGE: If you don't say you'll marry me I'll hang myself from that tree in front of your house.
CLEVER DICK GIRL: You know my father doesn't like you hanging around.

BOY: Darling, how could I ever leave you?
CLEVER DICK GIRL: By bus, car, plane, train . . .

ALICE: Is your boyfriend clever?
CLEVER DICK GIRL: Clever? He couldn't tell which direction a lift was going even if he had two guesses.

GIRL: Have you ever had a hot, passionate, burning kiss?
CLEVER DICK GIRL: I did once. He'd forgotten to take the cigarette out of his mouth.

GIRL: Do you think I'll lose my looks as I get older?
CLEVER DICK: With a bit of luck, yes.

CLEVER DICK GIRL: Do you love me?
BOY: I would die for you.
CLEVER DICK GIRL: You're always saying that, but you never do it.

CLEVER DICK GIRL: You remind me of my favourite boxer.
BOY: Frank Bruno? Barry McGuigan?
CLEVER DICK GIRL: No. I think he's called Rover.

CLEVER DICK: You look like an Italian dish.
GIRL: Madonna? Sophia Loren?
CLEVER DICK: No, macaroni cheese.

BOY: May I hold your hand?
CLEVER DICK GIRL: No thanks, it isn't heavy.

GIRL: Now we've decided to get engaged, I hope you'll give me a ring?
CLEVER DICK: Of course – what's your number?

GIRL: Did you miss me while I was away?
CLEVER DICK: Were you away?

GIRL: How do you like me?
CLEVER DICK: As girls go, you're fine. And the sooner you go, the better.

FRIEND: My girlfriend's as pretty as a flower.
CLEVER DICK: A cauliflower?

BOY: I've been told I have an infectious smile.
CLEVER DICK GIRL: In that case, don't stand too close to me.

CLEVER DICK: There are times when I really like you.
GIRL: When is that?
CLEVER DICK: When you're not yourself!

CLEVER DICK TO GIRLFRIEND: I'd like to pay you a compliment . . . but I can't think of one.

CLEVER DICK: Since we met, I can't eat or drink.
GIRL: Why not?
CLEVER DICK: I'm broke!

GIRL AT CINEMA: I love you so much I've got a cold, slithery feeling down my neck.
CLEVER DICK: So *that's* where my Cornetto went!

BOY: Oh darling, what would it take to make you give me a kiss?
CLEVER DICK GIRL: An anaesthetic.

BOY: Looks aren't everything.
CLEVER DICK GIRL: In your case they aren't anything.

GIRL: What about Danny? What do you think of his looks?
CLEVER DICK GIRL: I don't mind him looking — it's his face I can't stand!

CLEVER DICK: I can't leave you.
GIRL: Do you love me so much?
CLEVER DICK: It's not that. You're standing on my foot.

GIRL: I like nightlife . . .
CLEVER DICK: Owls, rodents, badgers, bats . . .

GIRL: Say you love me! Say you love me!
CLEVER DICK: You love me!

BOY: Would you marry the biggest idiot on earth?
CLEVER DICK GIRL: Oh, Fred, this comes so suddenly!

GIRL: I love men who are frank.
CLEVER DICK: Too bad, my name is Jonathon.

CLEVER DICK GIRL: The moment you kissed me I knew it was puppy love.
BOY: Why was that?
CLEVER DICK GIRL: Your nose was cold.

GIRL: Do you ever think of me?
CLEVER DICK: Yes, but I'd hate to tell you what.

BOY: What would you say if I asked you to marry me?
CLEVER DICK GIRL: Nothing. I can't talk and laugh at the same time.

BOY: I would go to the end of the earth for you!
CLEVER DICK GIRL: Yes, but would you stay there?